LIFE SKILLS

FOR TWEENS

TORY HUNT

ISBN-13: 979-8-9850464-6-5 (paperback)

TABLE OF CONTENTS

INTRODUCTION

"Good habits formed in youth make
all the difference." — Aristotle

For me, middle school was a confusing experience. Maybe it's called "middle" because one can easily get caught up in the middle of just anything. I want to be independent, but whenever my parents are away from home, I don't know how to cook and wash the laundry. It scares me to think ahead of living without them, but I also want to get away once they start nagging when I'm late for school and watching TV for a long time. Why do they have to watch over me all the time and track my activities?

Their endless questions about what I was doing in school sometimes tested my patience. When that happened, I would hide in my room and shut the door behind me. I wanted to be alone and at peace with myself. But even my "self" wouldn't allow it . . . the emotional struggle was still there.

The emotions added to all the other physical changes I was going through was just too much. I didn't even understand myself, didn't know why I felt the way I did, and yet, they expected me to understand them, read their minds, and do things the way they expected. I can understand most kids talking about how unreasonable their parents were.

I love my parents—there's no question about that—but I wasn't too happy when they treated me like a five-year-old kid. They would set confusing rules they couldn't even follow, like how important it is to be honest, then freaked out when I told them I took five dollars because I wanted to buy something.

It was even harder for me to deal with other kids in school. My life in middle school was challenging. I was shy and withdrawn because I always felt like I didn't fit in. I always compared things I didn't have with other kids in my class, feeling like I came up short of anything.

The first day in school for me was always the worst. I was scared to meet new kids and teachers. Everyone stared at me when our teachers asked us to introduce ourselves in class. I hated to raise my hand to answer a question my teacher asked even if I knew the answer. Still, I felt proud when I heard my name called to answer it, and I did!

I would get confused when almost everyone was talking about social media –TikTok, Facebook, Instagram, Twitter, Reddit, and so on because I didn't have any, and my parents wouldn't allow it. I had no idea how these kids could have social media accounts when minors weren't even allowed to have them.

I listened to kids in school bullying others and talking about things only adults should do. It could be one reason why I didn't have any friends. I became worried that all kids in my class were the same. They were out to hurt others or make them a laughingstock.

I realized I'd go to high school soon, which meant freedom. I'd soon be away from those troubling kids. I looked forward to the new life ahead, but was also afraid to face another level of challenges. What if high school kids were worse? What if I couldn't cope with the academic challenges? Could I just quit and go back?

Middle school was not my favorite time, however, this experience is all in the past now. It was a part of my childhood experience. Looking back, I am thankful for all these challenges because they were a part of me and helped me look for ways to improve myself and become what I am today. The most important thing is that I learned some essential life lessons from these years.

Be mindful of the things you do, especially on social media. Being visible on the internet does not only make you popular to influence others. It can also make you fall prey to evil characters. Bullying today is not only done physically: There are people who can even bully your online, which is called cyberbullying. As these social media sites showcase everything about you — from your personal information, location, and connections, you will never know what they can do to harm you. Listen to your parents and be wise and cautious when forming social bonds.

Take your time with things. Life has different stages for growth and development, whether physical, emotional, or mental. Take life as it is while you go through all those transformations. Remember not to dwell too much on high school or college while still in middle school. You have enough time to think about those things later. Instead, take advantage of those moments when you are with your family and enjoy the love and warmth they provide instead of getting overwhelmed by emotions and changes. They are your parents, and their presence in your life has a purpose.

Be nice. It pays to be friendly to your parents, siblings, other kids, or even yourself. You may not see its effect today, but being nice paves the way for better relationships in all aspects of life.

As you transition to the different stages in life, you will need essential life skills to help you navigate through your teenage years and beyond. You will need to learn the skills required to develop a career, deal with people, make decisions, and deal with everyday situations.

Most importantly, remember that you are unique and different. You have weaknesses and strengths. You have dreams and aspirations. However, your life is in your hands. The world is full of opportunities, and you have the power to create the kind of life you want to have. Your future life will depend on how you handle it today, and the life skills you will acquire are your best tools to live a happy and successful life. That's where this book comes in. This book is designed to help equip you with vital life skills that will propel you into your teenage years, and beyond.

Having strong life skills comes with many benefits. Some of the most important ones are:

- You will be able to handle difficult situations with ease
- You will be more confident in yourself and develop good behavior

- You will be able to achieve your goals and dreams
- You will have better relationships with others
- You will motivate yourself to become the best version of yourself
- You will make use of information in making good choices

Each chapter of this book will include tips, illustrations, activities, and real-life examples to help you understand and apply the life skills we discuss. So, let's get started!

If you're ready to embrace your teen and young adult years with a self-reliant attitude, dive in and learn how to accomplish the skills you need to achieve confidence, independence, and success!

CHAPTER 1

STUDY SKILLS: LEARNING IS FUN

"Success is no accident. It is hard work, perseverance,
learning, studying, sacrifice, and most of all, love
of what you are doing or learning to do."
— Pelé, Brazilian pro footballer

Success is not easy. You can earn success with hard work,
loving what you want to do, and having a strong
determination that one day, you will achieve your goal.
Without these traits, it will be hard for you to attain success. If
you do, your success may be temporary and will not stand the
test of time.

If you want to achieve something, there are valuable life skills
that you need to learn. Life skills are a set of basic skills that you
develop through learning and direct experience. These skills will

help you effectively handle problems and challenges you encounter every day.

Life skills include managing emotions, health, money, relationships, and school performance. Your ability to master them can improve your emotional balance, health, and independence.

Learning and knowledge help build the foundation for life skills. Because learning skills involve studying, you must not just study just because your parents asked you to, but also study hard to reap the benefits of learning.

WHAT IS STUDYING HARD AND WHY IT IS IMPORTANT

Studying hard is when you spend a good amount of time and energy learning and understanding so that you can accomplish something you want, such as a good grade on a test. You study hard when you try to read, practice, and memorize the information you want. Studying is about quality learning and not just quantity. Even though you might not particularly like a subject, you should explore all of them. Try to enjoy the act of studying and learning, as nothing will get into your mind if you don't love what you do, even if you spend long hours studying.

Why Do You Need to Study Hard?

You may not be eager to study hard because you don't understand why you have to learn what you think is the hard way. But there are significant reasons your parents are sending you to school to learn.

#1—Studying Hard Sharpens Your Brain

Your brain develops as you study. Your brain is elastic and continues to grow and expand depending on how much information you put into it: Reading can help your brain grow. Developing good reading habits while you're still young will help your brain grow into an enormous container of knowledge.

While you study, it prepares you for your future life. Lessons you learn in school are meant to prepare you for life. Studying hard allows you to acquire the skills you need to meet life's challenges and to be successful.

#2 —Studying Hard Makes You Hard-Working

Studying hard develops in you the habit of working hard. Diligence in your studies can earn you good grades and a scholarship when you get ready for college. Students who also work hard for their studies have a great chance of getting excellent jobs because of their exemplary academic performance.

When you put hard work into your studies, your mental development increases, and so do your reading, communication, and reading skills.

#3 —Studying Hard Helps You Land Your Dream Job

As you study hard for your dreams, you discover your interest and create career goals. While studying, you develop your interest in some areas and are motivated to learn more about them. Once you graduate from college or university, what you worked hard for will result in getting your dream job.

#4 —Studying Hard Empowers You

Studying hard empowers you with the wisdom, knowledge, skills, and values needed to become a productive citizen. It opens job opportunities, improves mental health, and promotes environmental care, cooperation, and unity.

STUDY SKILLS YOU NEED TO HAVE

Are you striving to be a successful student? It may be challenging, as it requires dedication and hard work. However, we have a study guide to help you learn how to study more effectively. It will help your academic performance and benefit you in all aspects of learning for the rest of your life!

Study Skills Checklist

All individuals are unique and have their differences. This is true even in their style of studying. You must know what works best for you so you can reap the full benefits of learning. To get started, try to answer the following study skills checklist. It will be the basis of your study habits and attitudes. Through self-assessment, you will know what study skills areas you need to address.

1. Y__ N__ I am spending more time learning than I need to.

2. Y__ N__ I'm used to cramming the night before our test.

3. Y__ N__ If I spend much time with friends, I only have a little time for studying. When I spend more time studying, I have less time with my friends.

4. Y__ N__ I'm used to studying with TV or radio and listening to music.

5. Y__ N__ I find it hard to understand the significance of what I'm studying.

6. Y __N__ I easily get distracted while studying.

7. Y__ N__ Whenever I'm in class, I would either daydream, draw, or fall asleep.

8. Y__ N__ I do not usually review my notes in preparation for exams.

9. Y__ N__ Seldom do I keep up with my assignments and therefore, I often have to cram.

10. Y__N__ I study a lot in preparation for a test, but my mind goes blank when I'm taking it.

11. Y__ N__ I wish I could read as quickly as others.

12. Y__ N__ I face difficulty answering essay tests despite being well prepared.

13. Y__ N__ I usually do my assignments and reports at the last minute.

14. Y__ N__ I typically get lost in preparation and need help getting the key concepts and main ideas.

15. Y__ N__ I easily get overwhelmed with assignments and projects and struggle to get started.

16. Y__ N__ Organizing my thoughts in writing is challenging.

17. Y__ N__ I'm consistent in my reading speed, regardless of the difficulty level and familiarity with the text I'm reading.

18. Y__ N__ I have a disorganized way of studying, as I only do it before a test.

19. Y__ N__ I need help identifying what is essential in reading.

20. Y__ N__ When I get to the end of my reading, I can't remember anything.

Listed here below are categories for self-help studies. If you have answered one YES or less to these questions, it means you are skillful in certain areas, but by answering YES more than two or more times in any of these categories, we recommend that you follow our directions to help you improve your skills in these areas.

- Time scheduling (1)(2)(3)
- Concentration (4)(6)(7)
- Listening and Note-Taking (5) (8)
- Studying (9)(14)(20)
- Reading (11)(17)(19)
- Exams (12)(10)(18)
- Writing (13)(15)(16)

Explore Your Learning Style

Because everyone has a different learning style, discovering what works best for you can be an advantage. When you understand your learning style better, you can find ways to improve its rate and quality. Understanding your learning style can also improve your understanding of yourself and others.

Let's talk about the different learning styles.

The most widely recognized learning styles are those of the VARK model, which stands for

Visual	Learning through seeing	
Auditory	Learning through hearing	
Reading/Writing	Learning through reading and writing	
Kinesthetic	Learning through doing and moving	

It can be frustrating to be in a class, knowing you need to absorb what is being discussed, but struggling to do so. Just remember, this challenge is not a reflection of how smart you are—it's about learning styles. The teacher may need to use a different style than what suits you best. For example, if your learning style is auditor and your teacher provides you with reading resources and asks you to read and write an essay based on them, you may struggle more than necessary, because reading and writing are not your preferred learning style.

People usually have a combination of these learning styles. It's best to understand what works for you and find ways to use your learning styles.

Another learning style theory is the Memletics which uses the VARK Model and adds the following categories:

Verbal	Learning through speaking	
Logical	Learning through logic and reasoning. These learners are good at mathematics.	
Social	Learning through group interaction	

Understanding these learning styles to know what suits you best is helpful, but you must also be careful not to limit yourself by your learning style. Just take what you can learn out of it, but never allow it to overcome your thoughts and limit what you can do.

Study Consistently

If you have a habit of studying the night before the test, it's time to stop. You will lose sleep, which can cloud your mind on exam day. Instead, have consistent study habits. Don't waste another day cram studying everything in one session. Shorter yet regular study periods are more effective, and they are less stressful.

1. Habits of Highly Successful Students: Have a Regular Study Schedule

Successful students have a regular study schedule and stick to it! By setting aside time to study either daily or a few days every week to review your lessons, you will develop this study habit that will eventually ensure your success.

2. Set a Goal for Each Study Time

You need to set goals in order for your study to be more effective. What do you hope to achieve when studying? For example, let's say your goal is to understand the concept you need to learn and apply it. Ask someone to explain if you can't understand it by reading through the textbook.

3. Start With the Most Difficult Subject

When doing your assignment, you must start with the one that needs more time and energy. After you have completed it, the rest will be easy. Doing it this way will improve your study and make it more effective.

4. Review Your Notes First

Taking notes in class is important so you can have them when studying. Review all your notes before doing your assignment so you can complete your assignment. Checking your notes before each study session will help you recall what you have learned in class, making your studying targeted and effective.

5. Avoid Distractions

You can easily get distracted, so make sure that the TV, radio, cell phones, and other video and audio devices are turned OFF.

Studying will be ineffective if you are disturbed or distracted, so make sure your place of study is free of background noise.

6. Join a Group Study

There are three benefits to joining a study group.

- You can get help from others when you need help understanding something from your lesson.
- You can teach others as well.

- You can complete your assignment in less time.

For the session to be successful, group members come prepared to study. In other words, they must complete any necessary reading prior to the study session and bring their course materials, notes, and textbooks.

7. Spend Your Weekend Reviewing

It's easy to retain what you have learned if you go over your notes and other resources during weekends when you're relaxed. Building this habit will also prepare you for the incoming week's lessons which are usually related to what you have learned the week before.

By developing these habits, we are confident that you will soon see improvements in your academic performance.

STUDY MOTIVATIONAL TIPS, TRICKS, AND HACKS

Are you easily distracted when studying? You're not alone. Some kids study for a few minutes but get lost in social media networks. If you're like this, you need some motivation to get back into your study mode, especially when a test is coming.

There's no one-size-fits-all study motivation strategy. Try finding what works for you. We have a list of motivational ideas to keep you back on track. Try them and find out what works for you!

Finding a Good Location

Finding an excellent location is the first thing you do when you want to study, unless you want to be distracted and unable to concentrate on what you are about to review.

Use Digital Blockers

Your most significant distraction when studying is digital, so why not use a digital app to fight it? There are available tools online for your desktop and phone. They can block whatever app or website is distracting you. So if TikTok, Facebook, or Instagram suck up most of your time, stop them while you study. AppBlock and Freedom are some of these blocking tools.

Adopt the Pomodoro Technique

The Pomodoro Technique is a study technique that aims to improve your study habits. The method is simple. Just follow these steps.

1. Have a 25-minute study time

2. Take 5-10 minutes break

3. Repeat these two steps four times

4. You can take longer breaks

You may create changes to this technique, like shortening the time intervals or repeating the process three times instead of four. You will need a timer to keep track of your study time and breaks. During your breaks, exercise is a great way to keep your blood running and keep you motivated to return to your study time. If you are using app blockers, they work well with the Pomodoro Technique.

Reward Yourself

After finishing your study session, reward yourself with something you love, like a box of chocolates, a ticket to your favorite pop star concert, or a day out with friends.

To motivate yourself to study well, think of a reward that can pressure you to do your best. You may receive your prize, let's say, after passing your test with a high score. Your parents can even join in to add more to the motivation; for example, they can treat you to a restaurant when you reach a goal.

The bottom line is to personalize your reward for it to be effective. Only set up a reward that will be possible for you to get. Similarly, only create a reward that you can accomplish easily.

Time Management for Better Study

It is easy to waste time, especially when you feel you have nothing else to do. You will most likely put off study time, thinking you'll have more time to do it later. This is called procrastination, and it is not a good habit to develop. However, when you know there's a lot to do in a day, you tend to focus on completing the task before you. Setting a schedule with tasks and deadlines can help you manage your time.

Consider these strategies to avoid wasting time:

- Prepare your term calendar for all tasks and activities.
- Make a monthly schedule
- Make a daily schedule

In order to be effective in your study, the key is to study smarter, not harder. Some students can perform well in school with minimum effort because of their effective study habits. Consider these study habits if you want to succeed.

Structured Procrastination

Believe it or not, you can use your time-wasting habit. This concept is called structured procrastination, which Professor John Perry of Stanford University developed.

According to this concept, if you procrastinate, you tend to tackle easy tasks first and put off bigger and more challenging tasks. You can be motivated to do timely, challenging, and demanding tasks as long as these tasks are your way of doing something more important. To make this work, think of tasks that are far more important than studying. It will make the task of studying way less easy and less important for you to do. And because you think of it as a minor task, you are more likely to complete it.

The Cornell System for Taking Notes

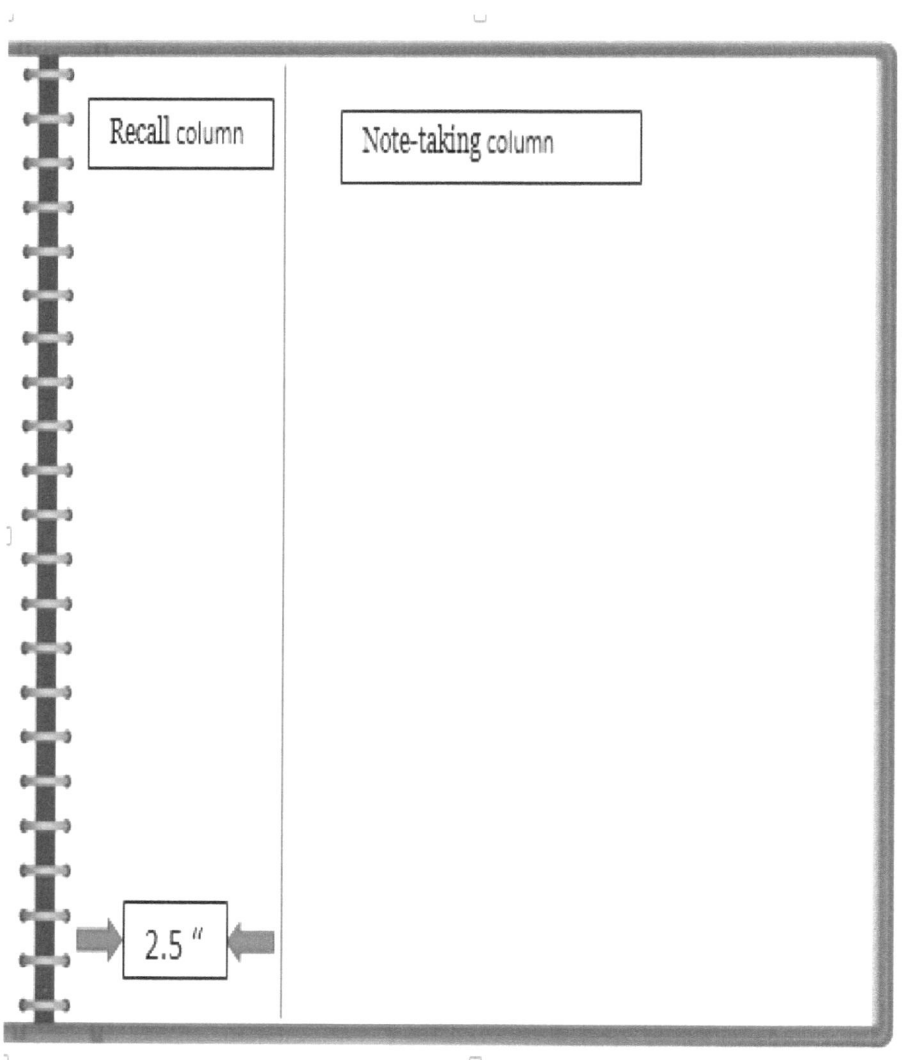

The Cornell System is a method of taking notes which allows students to save time while maximizing the effectiveness of taking notes. This system was devised by a professor at Cornell University named Walter Pauk in the 1950s.

Here are the steps involved in taking notes using the Cornell System.

Step #1 – Divide a Page of Your Notebook Into Two Columns

- Use a loose-leaf notebook for taking notes. You will use only one side of the page.

- Two and a half inches from the left, draw a vertical line. The first column is the recall column of your notes, and the second column to the right is where you will be writing all your lecture notes.

- Take note of the keywords and phrases using the recall column.

Step#2 – Take Notes Using the Right Column

- Capture ideas and concepts from the lecture and write them down in the note-taking column. Be as brief as you can.

- Use abbreviations to save time and write as clearly as you can.

- Note relevant questions and keywords in the recall column to help you later when you review your notes.

Step #3 – Review Notes Within the Day

- After the lecture, review what you have written and ensure that everything you have noted is written clearly.

- Add more keywords and ideas you can remember in the recall column.

- Read again what you have written in the right column, reflect on what the teacher had discussed, and try to say them in your own words while covering your notes in the right column.

- Make the recall column your guide while reciting the lecture.

Checklist to Improving Your Note-Taking

1. Make clear and accurate notes

2. Come to class prepared

3. Compare notes

4. Minimize distractions

5. Organize notes using the Cornell System

6. Use abbreviations and symbols for speed writing

7. Write clearly

8. Review your notes

9. Write down questions

10. Avoid digital notes

11. Use effective methods like the outline method and the charting method.

Improving Your Memory

It is common for students to need help remembering information. Since exams are designed to test what you have placed out of your lessons learned in class and personal study, memory retention is closely linked to academic success. Remembering what you have learned is essential when looking for a job after graduation.

You may have noticed why complex video games are easy to remember, but multiplication tables are not. If this sounds like you, then you're not alone. Every normal kid has experienced this.

However, some strategies will help improve your memory retention and recall, teaching you how to recall and memorize important information.

It is easier to remember information when you can picture them in your mind. This method is helpful when learning confusing subjects, not abstract ones. To apply this strategy, create images that you can relate to the abstract idea or concept. Visualizing them will increase the likelihood that your mind will easily recall them.

Improve your recall ability through the following:

- Teach others, as in a group study
- Compare and analyze resource materials

Critical Thinking Skills

Critical thinking is the ability to evaluate and understand logical relationships between ideas. Understanding these relationships allows you to find answers or solutions, draw conclusions, or create sound arguments. It helps you analyze other people's opinions or explanations to determine whether they were developed through sound reasoning.

Critical thinking requires connecting crucial ideas and concepts. It involves solving problems systematically. Part of this skill consists in prioritizing the best ideas for your arguments.

Students who constantly hone their critical thinking skills become better prepared to deal with various issues they face in school and life. They can skillfully create new concepts based on ideas and information they've previously learned.

Learning the Basics

Before finishing high school, you should refine several advanced critical thinking skills. They will help you immensely during your college years. These skills include the following:

1. Identification

Recognizing a problem, the factors that influence it, and the effects of it are essential to the critical thinking process. Specifically, this skill allows you to see and weigh a particular problem, driving you to think further about how to solve it. These questions will guide you in identifying and learning about a problem:

- What is the problem?
- Why is it happening?
- What is the outcome of this problem?

2. Research

When you have identified a problem, you can start studying it. This is what you call research. How much research is involved depends on the scope of the problem—the more complicated the situation, the more materials you may need to reference and address it.

Research is important to prove an idea or concept. You need to explore more and look for evidence to back up your claim instead of accepting it without any investigation.

3. Recognizing Biases

Everyone has a bias, regardless of age and life achievements. As a learner, you must be able to recognize bias in the materials you're studying. This is because authors tend to write content that may favor a particular viewpoint. Knowing how to spot biases can help you decide whether or not to trust a source.

Furthermore, you should be able to examine your biases. Learn how to write objectively. Avoid focusing only on your set of opinions and perspectives. Challenging your point of view and the evidence you have read is part of the critical thinking process.

4. Making Inferences

You should be able to assess the outcome based on the body of evidence you've seen. However, you can only draw the correct conclusions sometimes. If this happens, all you need to do is review existing evidence and study any new information.

5. Establishing Relevance

How relevant is the information you use to support your argument or conclusion? You have to establish this connection. Sorting through your primary and supporting documents to identify the data that strongly supports your claims is an example of this skill. Becoming more proficient in this area means cutting the time spent dealing with unnecessary information.

6. Curbing Your Curiosity

One of the biggest challenges you have to face is learning to discipline your curiosity. It sounds ironic because curiosity fuels your drive to explore things. However, the constant need to establish relevance is the key to recognizing where you should draw the line.

An uncontrolled curiosity can lead you to do time-wasting research that will have no result. The more skilled you become at following specific research paths, the more you can focus on relevant information and finding evidence to support your research.

Effective Listening Skills

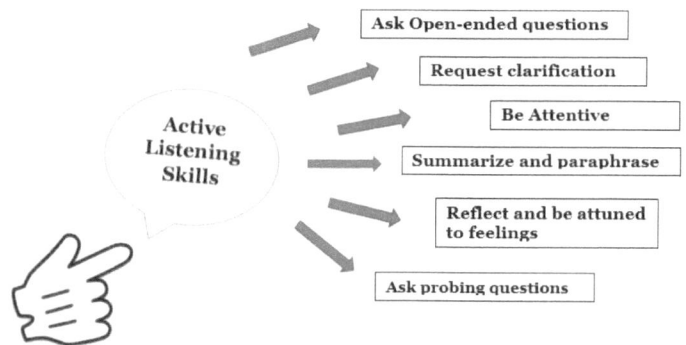

Good learners are attentive listeners. As a student, you spend more time listening to lectures. Some students believe they listen well. But listening is different from hearing. You may be hearing information, but if it fails to reach your brain, it is unprocessed and converted into knowledge.

Here are some strategies to help you improve your listening power to be more attentive.

- Pay Attention and Concentrate. Focus on the message and understand the main idea.
- Engage With Your Instructor. Ask questions or clarify things that aren't clear to you.
- Take Care of Your Health.

Critical Reading Skills/Strategies

When it comes to learning, students like you must know how to perform a more active form of reading known as **critical reading**. Critical reading is a practice that allows readers to deeply understand the material they are reading. It urges them to analyze, evaluate, and interpret the materials.

Critical Reading Structure

There are six elements that differentiate critical reading from regular reading.

- Purpose
- Activity
- Focus
- Questions
- Direction
- Response

Regular Reading vs. Critical Reading

	Regular Reading	Critical Reading
Purpose	Get the basic idea	Assess, understand, and judge the content

Activity	Absorb the contents— More relaxed	Constantly evaluate the contents. Look for supporting evidence to know if the text is valid
Focus	Pay attention to what the text is all about	Determine how logical the argument is
Questions	Simple	Critical

Sample questions:

Regular Reading	Critical Reading
What is the content all about?	How was the argument made?
What information can I obtain by reading this text?	What choices were involved in the content presented in this material?
	What reasoning did the author use?
	What were the author's inferences in this writing?

	Regular Reading	Critical Reading
Direction	Goes with the flow of the text— more relaxed	Greatly depends on the set of questions that come up during the evaluation
Response	You accept that the content is true	You probe, analyze, and make logical reasoning or arguments

Strategies for Reading Textbooks

Reading textbooks may not be exciting. However, understanding how to read and use them effectively can be a great tool in achieving your academic goals. Below are the steps on how to improve your textbook reading skills:

BEFORE READING	
Preview the Text	• Review all chapter and sub-chapter headings. • Skim over photos, illustrations, graphs, diagrams, etc. • Read bold or italicized texts. • Review the chapter summary. • Review questions by the end of each chapter.

Ask Questions 	• Write down anything you want to ask before starting to read the text. • Turn chapter and subchapter headings into questions.
WHILE READING	
Reflect 	• Answer the questions you had during the preview. • Read the text out loud. • Visualize presented information and concepts.
Select and Highlight 	• Identify important concepts. Underline them and put "Q" in the margin. • Circle important vocabulary words. Write short meanings in the margin. • Make visual aids, pictures, diagrams, tables, and graphs. • Write a summary of ideas and themes.

AFTER READING	
Share	• Read and tell what you've learned to someone else. • Explain what you've read out loud. • Join a study group.
Review	• Spend at least 20 to 30 minutes reviewing your notes within the day. • Recite the main topics and key takeaways. • Spend at least 10 minutes each week reviewing your notes, especially the highlighted parts.

Below are a few more things to consider in textbook reading:

What to Read
Know what texts you should focus on to save time and energy.

Study Location
Find a peaceful and stress-free location where you can concentrate.

Reading Schedule
Avoid reading late at night. Read for about 30 to 45 minutes and take a short break to refresh your mind.

How to Retain the Information
Read out loud and discuss what you've read with your study group or partner.

More tips when you find textbook reading quite challenging:

Change Positions
Stand up and move around occasionally.

Recite
Reading out loud improves retention and comprehension. Read the same passage several times to memorize and fully understand the information.

Look for Keywords
Remove the adjectives and adverbs to understand the main thought.

Use Markings
Underline or mark the text you don't understand. List them so you'll know what questions to ask in class.

Search Online
Search the web for additional information.

Refresh
Take a break if you find yourself tired and unable to focus.

TEST-TAKING GUIDES

Now, it's time to deal with tests, as tests are what most students are afraid of. Taking a test itself is a skill. Learning how to take a test is vital to your education, and we need to explore strategies and tips for taking tests and improving your academic performance.

Simple Strategies for Improving Test Performance

You might say improving your test performance puts you in a very tight spot, but it's not that hard. Try practicing the basic study strategies that you'll find here. One or two strategies, when applied, will surely increase your performance. Even better, make it a habit to try all these strategies starting on day 1 of your class. Your academic and test performance will improve significantly.

TYPES OF TESTS

Below are various types of tests and how to cope with them.

Short-Answer Test

As you approach the end of a lesson, your teacher may give unannounced quizzes or short tests to assess if you have learned anything from what has been discussed. To prepare yourself, here are some tips.

Study for Understanding

You must understand the concept of what you have learned. Even if you fail to remember a term or memorize information, understanding the course material and ideas will help you develop an answer that will likely get you either partial or full credit. So when preparing for a short answer test, ensure you understand and not just memorize.

Test Yourself

Try to guess what type of concepts the test will cover and try to practice to prepare yourself. If you can get access to previous class tests, it's a good idea to familiarize yourself with the concepts.

Use Flashcards

Flashcards prove to be beneficial to many students. Create flashcards. Write a term on one side, a definition, and other facts on the other.

Read all Instructions First

It is essential to understand the instructions before answering. Make sure you follow the instructions, as this can affect the validity of your answers.

Answer the Easy Questions First

Quizzes have limited time. Answer the easy one first. Don't get stuck up in one question, but move to the next one. You can get back to it later if there is still time. If you don't know the answer, make an educated guess.

Read Each Question Twice

Read each question twice before answering. It is common for a short-answer question to require multiple answers. For example, compare A with B. List their differences. If you are in a rush and read only the first part, it will affect your answers and cause you to miss half of the point for this number.

Clarify

If you find the question confusing, it won't hurt you to ask for clarification. However, do not ask your classmate sitting next to you. Instead, go to your teacher.

Be Thorough and Concise

As much as possible, be brief and concise in your answers. Your answer should include just enough information to answer the question accurately and completely. You can provide short solutions. Most of the time, long explanations that don't prove a point will only cause you to lose points in the same way that a short incorrect one will have the same effect.

True or False Test

You may love answering the true or false test, but do you know these questions are tricky? Here are some tricks to help improve your ability to answer true and false questions.

41

View Each Question as If it is True

If you view each question as accurate and then closely examine it to find its flaw, it will be easier to determine if it is true or false. Discovering that one part of the statement is false means the whole message false.

For a statement to be accurate, all facts contained must be correct and not have any false information.

Essay Test

Unlike other test types, essay tests require you to answer the questions based on how you understand the lesson. Essay tests are easy if you know the concept and review it before the test. If not, consider the following strategies to help you improve your performance on essay tests.

Read the Directions

It's essential to understand first what is being asked. Most often, the teacher is looking for a specific answer. Only assume you know the answer after reading the whole instruction or question. If there is something you can't understand, then clarify it with your teacher.

Organize Your Thoughts

Before starting your essay:

- Organize your thoughts.
- Create an outline in your mind of what you want to write.
- Start with the main idea before adding details.

You don't need to make it long, but if you can give as many points to support your answer, the better. Your teacher will know through your replies that you learned what was taught. However, only fill your answer with details that are correct or related to the topic.

Be Concise

A typical answer should be at most 800 words or less than 200 (2-8) paragraphs, as more does not mean better. Instead, focus on the substance.

Your answer should have three parts:

- Introduction
- Body
- Conclusion

The body usually consists of two to six paragraphs. Use paragraphs to separate ideas and make sure that there is a smooth flow of information.

Review What You Wrote

If you still have time left, review and make changes when needed. Check your grammar, as it is common to make mistakes when focusing on the content of your answer rather than how you use words.

Open-Book Test

In this type of exam, you are allowed to open your notes, textbooks, and other reference materials while you are taking your exam because this exam is more challenging than the usual tests you have. It focuses on higher learning and requires you to evaluate and analyze information rather than memorize and remember it. Here are ways to help you deal with open-book exams.

Prepare

This exam tests your understanding of the subject matter, not your memory recall and retention. You must study and prepare beforehand.

Because exams have limited time, opening references can even be an advantage. Organize your resource materials and ensure you're familiar with their content to save time finding the correct references. The more reference material you bring, the less time you will waste finding what you need. It may help to outline your references so you can quickly find what you will be looking for.

To prepare, identify key concepts and terms that will likely appear on your exams, and using your notes, identify points that your teacher is more likely to include in the test. Once the test begins, your primary concern is to find the information you need in your references. You may bookmark pages for easy access but remember that you should come to take the test only after reviewing all fundamental concepts and topics taken from lectures.

Avoid Copying

Never copy anything from the book. Your teacher is more concerned about knowing what you have learned. It won't help you to rely heavily on the book. You may base your answer on the text to support your analysis, but do not plagiarize it.

Lastly, like other tests, be aware of the length of time you spend answering each question.

STUDY SKILL RESOURCES BY SUBJECT

Computer Skills

Computer-based skills are mostly elective at the elementary, high school, and college levels. However, some institutions require their students to complete at least an introductory, if not fundamental, computer course before graduation because using computers is now a basic necessity in education.

Here are some tips to start your computer learning:

Choose the right path before anything else. Most students get fascinated by video games, eventually leading them to get computer-related skills, only to get dismayed after learning that they have to spend most of their time programming. Computed programming is not a miserable course, though it requires more time and attention. In other words, if you like games, you can choose different career paths, such as Graphic Arts, Technical Writing, Business Management, or Game Design.

Study Math. If you want to learn Computer Programming, you need to study math, or anything related could pose a challenge. Computer hardware engineers and researchers also do math-based calculations whenever they design machines.

Avoid working solo whenever possible. Whether you are fixing computers or doing other computer-related work, it is good to work with a team rather than being solo. Knowing how to operate within groups is a must if you decide to work under a company in the future.

Don't stop learning. Education is constantly changing, which also applies to computer skills. Even though there are basics about computers that do not change, many things related to them can create a big change in a few years. Hence, you must update yourself about these things as much as possible.

English

Speaking this language might come naturally as breathing if you're a native speaker. However, it doesn't necessarily mean that you can also write English words without errors. It is due to this reason that even native speakers must study English to write their language effectively.

Read, read, read! This is the most effective means to study languages in their written form. Spending at least half an hour reading materials like books, newspapers, ads and other references will enrich your knowledge.

Be consistent. No one learns a whole language in just one sitting. In other words, as long as you're willing to learn English, you don't have to read an entire novel and finish it overnight. Always remember that studying little by little with proper comprehension is better than trying to learn everything in a single night.

Ask for help. If you want to improve your English more, ask for help from experts. It could be your English Teacher, tutor, or linguist. The goal should be to learn things you cannot understand or figure out yourself.

Take notes. Whenever you find something fascinating about English, it is recommended that you write it down. Writing not only improves your active listening skills; it also enables you to turn short-term memories into long-term ones.

History

Students usually find History boring, but it can be fun and exciting when approached with the right attitude. Learning history provides you with a knowledge of past events and will also prepare you for career opportunities in the future.

Here's how to study history more effectively:

Establish Connections between written facts. History is not just full of facts, events, and details. It also needs to be remembered in the proper chronological order, or your efforts in studying it will be meaningless. It will be like saying that

Richard the Lionheart was born during the Civil War or that the Pope has his headquarters in New York, which is one hundred percent wrong.

To remember which is which, you need to make distinct connections by writing every significant event in detail. Try understanding the big picture by analyzing the main event before connecting everything related to it. For example, as long as you can remember that Richard the Lionheart is a primary character in Medieval History, especially the Crusades, you can start from there by writing everything that happened in his time as much as possible.

Memorize the essential information. History is unique compared to other subjects because the most important events, names, and places will likely appear on your quizzes and tests. In other words, if you memorize those in detail, you will likely pass every quiz or test your teacher gives you. Moreover, history teachers tend to emphasize the topics that will probably appear in their tests, so make sure to take note of these things.

Take time to read. Despite the saying that winners wrote history, we cannot deny that the subject is mainly based on the common knowledge written and preserved for generations. To learn more, you need to read lots of books.

Watch movies. Some award-winning movies portraying historical events are entertaining and historically accurate. One good example is *Schindler's List*, which was about the History of Poland under German Occupation during World War II.

Mathematics

What makes mathematics different from other subjects is that you cannot become proficient by actively listening and reading about it. To learn from it, you need to do lots of homework and activities, or else you won't be doing any calculations correctly, even if you memorize the formulas by heart. In other words, math is a subject that rewards both the talented and those willing to work for it.

Tips for Learning Math

Here are the tips for studying and learning math effectively:

Learn and perfect the basics. Unlike other subjects, math is sequential. In other words, the basic principles such as addition, subtraction, multiplication, and division are still applicable at higher levels like arithmetic, algebra, geometry, and trigonometry. The time will come when you need to memorize many equations and formulas, but if you don't master the basics, you will have difficulties reaching the following levels.

Memorize and initiate the correct formulas correctly.
Any student can memorize a formula or two, and that's a given fact. However, only a few pay close attention to applying it correctly. Just like with cooking, even if you have the right formula, the results will always be wrong if you do not do the mathematical process correctly.

Enrich your math vocabulary. Math has its own set of vocabulary. When studying the subject, you might hear different words such as formula, equation, circumference, surface area, etc. At first, you might be baffled by it, but as your study progresses, you will get the hang of it.

Widen your comprehension. Studying and solving math problems requires lots of dedication and extensive comprehension ability. After all, you need to identify and understand the problem before applying the right solution to it. In other words, if you tend to have a short fuse and attention span, you won't be able to solve anything.

Double-check everything. Like other subjects, you must double-check everything whenever you solve math problems. This will ensure that you have completed all necessary details that might affect the outcome of your given solution.

Science

Science is a subject that encompasses several fields and has three distinct branches, namely: formal science, social science, and natural science. Depending on the branch of science you are studying, it might also require different types of note-taking. For example, social science requires intensive reading, so memorization and journaling are recommended, while physical sciences require taking pictures since it's composed chiefly of diagrams.

Here are the tips for studying science effectively:

Tips for Studying Science Effectively

Familiarize Yourself With the Terms. Every scientific area has a distinct terminology that needs memorizing. For example, organisms and genes often come up when you're studying biology, while elements and formulas are terms found in chemistry. Learning these terms before taking classes is very helpful since it can be confusing if your teacher uses this without your understanding.

Understand Scientific Concepts. Unlike terms, concepts are more complex since they are less defined, requiring you to take more notes. For example, mitosis and meiosis are terms, but they include a detailed process for DNA splitting or recombination and chromosomes.

Look for Visual Aids. When studying science, visual aids are recommended since most of its topics are not commonly known. For example, even if your science teacher tells you everything about cells, you will only get an idea about them if they show illustrations or visual aid.

Promote Hands-On Learning. It will be challenging for you to study science at home by just reading textbooks. Science requires a hands-on method and application of what you have learned to understand it completely. So, here's what you need to do.

Draw lots of diagrams. Diagrams represent information clearly and visually. They will help you visualize the structures and functions of different systems, parts, processes, cycles, etc.

Draw or Create Models. Some concepts are challenging to understand, like the solar system. You will only know how they are and why they matter if you can see a sample of their appearance.

Disassemble Parts. Sometimes, you can learn science at home by breaking things apart to see how these parts function together. You may cut a seed to see what's inside or a flower to see its parts. But remember, only disassemble gadgets or toys after asking your parents if you can do it.

Do Home Experiments. It is important to do hand-in experiments. Consider the following steps:

Watch a Video of an Experiment. When interested in experimenting, first find an instructional video on how to do it.

1. Understand how the experiments work before attempting to do them. It will save you time, money, and mess!

2. Take notes of the materials, directions, and results as you watch the video.

3. Find all the materials and equipment you will need. Make sure that everything is ready before you start your experiment.

Do the Experiment. Experimenting allows you to learn through trial and error. You will see how different variables can affect the result. Also, make a record of the various effects of your experiments. You may record it using video recording.

Learning skills are necessary to improve your academic performance in school as they prove to be the building blocks of your future success in many areas of life.

CHAPTER 2

HOUSEHOLD SKILLS

"One thing I think kids need to do is more chores and care for their rooms. Responsibilities are really important to start with. If they have animals, they have to feed them and care for them. That's the only way I think I could do it." — Faith Ford

Taking responsibility starts at home. If you want to grow up a responsible kid, you must practice being responsible in the place where you live. You can start by doing household chores like making your bed, cleaning your room, cooking, doing the laundry, and many more.

Doing household chores are necessary though they undoubtedly are energy and time-consuming. However, here are seven reasons why you should consider helping around your home:

1. Chores are life-skill teachers. You may be a kid for now, but you won't stay a kid all your life. When you finally move out of mom and dad's nest, you will eventually need to learn and do the cooking, budgeting, and laundry. Such essential life skills are only partially taught and learned at school, but you can learn and practice them in your home.

2. Chores encourage kids to become self-reliant and responsible. Do you want your parents or grandparents to see you as mature enough to be in charge of yourself even when you're young? Responsibility is the keyword here, and doing your assigned chores will help you become a more responsible person. Tasks that affect you personally, like doing your laundry or cleaning your room, can help you attain that, aside from being more self-reliant while you're at it.

3. Chores bring out teamwork. Household chores can bring out the model of being a productive team member for kids. Consider your family as a team where each member is accountable to one other. Consequences occur whenever a member doesn't meet other team members' expectations.

At an early age, learn these lessons at home to hone and strengthen teamwork skills for school or work (in the future). Also, a home is a more forgiving place whenever you happen to make mistakes.

4. Chores reinforce respect. The only time you'll finally learn to appreciate your parents' efforts in doing the hard work is when you experience it hands-on after moving out from the comfort of your home. However, if you were able to experience doing this housework even at a young age and in the vicinity of your home, it will be easier to get an insight of what is necessary to maintain a home. If you're assigned to clean the house, you'll become more sensitive to the messes you make and pay more respect to keeping your surroundings clean.

5. Chores aid in honing a solid work ethic. Work ethics are not only valued by teachers but also by employers. Doing chores is another simple way to instill this trait in yourself. For example, rewards like TV time or additional allowance come when you do your assigned house task. Your parents might even pay you for errands or chores done well. It may encourage you to work outside when you become a teen and lead to having a solid entrepreneurial inclination.

6. Chores teach skills in planning and time management. Though it may be difficult to fit chores into your daily schedule, chores can teach you good habits. Choosing and doing the right priorities first so you can manage your time wisely is an essential skill for work. True, it's hard to balance chores, social life, and school deadlines, but if you choose your responsibilities and set the right priorities first, you will be able to handle them in the future.

7. Chores also mean family bonding time. Believe it or not, chores can be your way of bonding time with your ever-busy parents. Usually, parents at home are preoccupied with chores, but if you help them with the chores around the house, you also get the chance to have memorable moments with them. It goes the same with the little ones who always want to give a hand to mom or dad. They feel essential and more confident after finishing their assigned task. Even moody teens may consider opening up to their parents while sharing a job.

HOW TO DO LAUNDRY

Doing laundry is a life skill you will inevitably use at some point in your life. After all, you will leave the nest someday, and mom won't be there to do the task on your behalf.

You may think that doing laundry is a complicated task. Rest assured that it isn't. Like any other skill, it's learnable.

Laundry Checklist

To summarize the steps involved in laundry cleaning, here's a simple guide that will help you remember them:

Pre-washing	• Shake them off-unball, unbundle, unroll • Sort them out-by color, fabric
Washing	• Do not overload • Apply detergent • Adjust settings • Start
Drying	• Check the lint tray • Shake out clothes before putting them into the dryer • User dryer sheets (optional) • Adjust settings • Start
Post Washing	• Fold or hang clothes • Place them in drawers and closets

Laundry Instructions

Below are six essential steps you should keep in mind to make the chore effortless:

Step 1: Shake Them Off!

You can find chaos in your laundry basket. Aside from dirt and unpleasant odor, you may notice how strange your clothes appear—entangled sleeves or rolled-up hem jeans. Some are bundled like balls of socks, underwear inside pants, or undershirts inside shirts.

The first step to making your laundry easy is to separate any combined layers and spread out anything rolled up.

Step 2: Sort Them Out

We don't want to ruin our favorite clothes. One of the best precautions to avoid this mishap is simple: never neglect to sort them out before washing them. So, one of the basic steps you must learn is to sort them out.

Start by separating the lights and darks since darker dyes can stain or discolor lighter fabrics. Separate your blacks, grays, navy, dark purples, and reds into one load. Put your pinks, yellows, light greens, light blues, and lavenders in another pile. Whites should go in a separate pile, but if you only have a few, mix them with your light-colored fabrics.

While at it, make sure to turn your clothes inside out. This way, you can protect your fabrics during the wash cycle, making them last longer.

Do Not Overload

You might think it's only logical to do one load to save time and energy. However, this could be counterproductive. Overloading can damage your washer's drum and decrease its efficiency. As a result, your clothes will not wash accordingly, and you will have to repeat the task. It also results in wasted soap, water, and energy. You will also lose time you could have spent on other activities.

Step 3: Apply Detergent

For beginners, an all-in-one pod is more practical. Although, of course, there's nothing wrong if your family uses powder or liquid detergents. When using powder or liquid detergents, you must read and follow the package instructions. Simple as it may be, following simple package instructions such as this helps you improve a critical life skill, namely, being able to follow directions.

Step 4: Adjust the Settings

There are warm, cold, and hot cycle options on your machine. If you have allergies and need to eliminate pollen and dust mites, choose the hot cycle. Just a little precaution: hot cycles can damage some types of fabrics. If you need help with what to do, ask your mom or dad about it.

Cold cycles are appropriate for almost all fabrics, especially those with dark color dyes. Fabrics loosen in hot water, allowing the dark dye to run. This causes the color of your clothes to fade, and you don't want that. Moreover, using the cold setting means you use less water and electricity.

After selecting the necessary settings, remember to press START.

Step 5: It's Time to Dry Them Up

While washing, check on your dryer machine and ensure the lint tray is empty. The lint tray catches the lint your clothes produce during the drying process. When the tray is full, it forces the dryer to use more electricity as the machine works harder. This also means that the drying time will be longer, and the longer the drying time, the more money goes down the drain.

Once you're ready to dry your clothes, shake out your clothes before putting them into the machine. Doing this step helps you avoid wrinkled clothes. It also helps cut down time on drying. You can also drop dryer sheets at this point to help reduce the static cling and make your clothes softer and more fragrant.

Choose the appropriate setting for your clothes. Generally, you use high heat for heavy fabrics such as towels, sweaters, and jeans. Use medium heat for synthetic fabrics and low for delicate ones like silk, chiffon, and wool.

Once everything is okay, don't forget to hit the START button.

Step 6: Put Them Back in Place

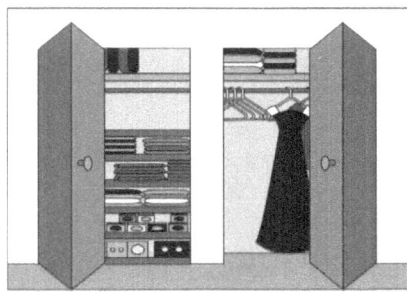

Finally, you have to get these clothes out of the dryer. Fold or hang them in your cabinet or clothes organizer.

Managing Your Expectations

Do you have to do this task impeccably, just like your mom does it? Of course not! You don't have to set your expectations high. You're still a child, and with that fact alone, you must give yourself some allowances.

If you spill some detergent, that's fine. If you forgot to shake out the clothes before putting them in the dryer, that's okay. It's also not the end if you cannot fold your clothes perfectly or mistakenly place your pajamas in your sock drawer.

The goal is to learn and practice what you've learned. It is a process, and you are allowed to make mistakes along that process. As time goes by, you will learn how to perfect the skill. You will eventually get to the point where you forget the awkward little things you did in the past. That's how it is. For now, enjoy learning.

HOW TO COOK SIMPLE MEALS

Cooking is one of the vital life skills you need to learn at some point in your life. Some boys may think that cooking is limited to females, but we beg to differ.

Cooking helps both girls and boys like you explore various skills and creativity. It also builds your confidence and lays the foundation for healthy eating habits. It enables you to explore your senses by recognizing and identifying different kinds of smell, taste, texture, and appearance.

Getting Started

Before proceeding to cook, there are crucial things you must do:

1. Properly wash your hands with soap and warm water.

2. Remember to tie your hair up if you have long hair.

3. Cover your mouth while coughing and sneezing, and wash your hands afterward.

4. Wash your hands after handling eggs, poultry, meat, or fish.

5. Immediately wash or clean items that come in contact with raw eggs, poultry, meat, or fish.

6. Discard any food item that falls on the floor.

7. Never use the utensil you used for cooking to taste the food because it causes contamination. Instead, use a separate spoon for tasting the food.

8. Make sure to keep your workstation clean and sanitized.

Keep these basic principles at heart so that they will become part of your good cooking habits.

Meanwhile, here are some easy recipes you can master in no time. And since it's your first time cooking, you can practice our recipes here with your parents. Cooking terms may also be new to you, so you need their help to follow instructions.

Basic Cooking Terms Commonly Used

Boil: Heat the liquid until it reaches boiling and creates bubbles.

Simmer: Heat the liquid to just below the boiling point.

Sauté: Briefly cook ingredients like garlic and onions in a little bit of oil over high heat.

Fry: Cooking food in hot oil or fat.

Marinate: Soaking meat or fish in a prepared marinade or mixture before cooking

Grill: Cooking form involving dry heat applied to the food surface.

Steam: Cooking over boiling water but not allowing your ingredients to be soaked in the water. Instead, they are held just above the water by a steamer basket.

Roast: A method of cooking using intense heat, which sears the outside of food, producing a nice, crunchy flavor.

Blanch: Cooking vegetables in boiling water very briefly to maintain color and crispness.

Baste: Brushing juices from the meat to keep it moist.

Pare: Peeling fruit or vegetable skin.

Season: Adding salt and pepper or other seasonings like spices and herbs.

Slice: Cutting food into neat, even pieces.

Cut: The act of slicing with a knife.

Dice: Cutting ingredients into cubes.

Julienne: Cutting ingredients into long, fine, even strips.

Chop: The general method of cutting food into bite-sized pieces.

Spaghetti

Servings: 4

Ingredients

- 2 x 800g can chopped tomatoes
- 1 large carrot, finely chopped
- 1 small onion, finely chopped
- 2 stalks of celery, finely chopped
- 2 cloves garlic, crushed
- ½ tsp. dried oregano
- 2 tbsp. butter
- ½ tbsp. olive oil

- 20 capers, halved

- Salt and pepper, to taste

Instructions

1. Prepare the spaghetti noodles according to the package instructions.

2. Preheat the pan over medium heat, then add the oil and butter. Melt the butter and add the chopped onion. Sauté for about 2 to 3 minutes until softened.

3. Add the garlic, carrots, and celery and cook until the carrots are tender. Remember to stir regularly to avoid burning.

4. Add the tomatoes, oregano, and capers, and then season with salt and pepper. Mix well.

5. Let the sauce cook for about 10 to 12 minutes. Serve with cooked spaghetti.

Creamy Potato Soup

Servings: 8

Ingredients

- 3 medium russet potatoes

- 2 cups whole milk

- 2 tbsp. butter

- Water

- Salt and pepper, to taste

Instructions

1. Wash, scrub, peel, and chop the potatoes. Add them to a medium soup pot and add water. Make sure that the water fully covers the potatoes.

2. Cook the potatoes for about 15 to 20 minutes or until you can easily cut one piece with a fork. Remove from the heat and carefully drain.

3. Add the milk and butter to the potatoes. Bring the pot back to the stove over medium heat. Cook for another 5 to 10 minutes or until the milk bubbles around the edges.

4. Turn off the heat and ladle into soup bowls. Before serving, add salt and pepper.

Quesadillas

Servings: 4

Ingredients

- 2 cups shredded cheese (mozzarella, cheddar, Mexican, or Monterey Jack)

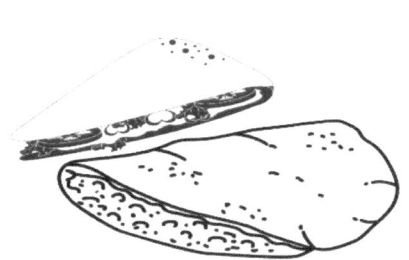

- 4 medium flour tortillas
- ½ tbsp. olive oil

Optional fillings:

Chicken: shredded rotisserie chicken or taco-seasoned chicken

Beef: taco-seasoned ground beef, diced tomatoes, avocado slices, black beans, and cheese

Mediterranean: diced tomatoes, onion slices, chopped spinach, shredded mozzarella, and feta cheese crumbles

Instructions

1. Spritz a large frying pan with olive oil and put it over medium-high heat for about 2 minutes.

2. Put the tortilla in the pan and let it warm for about 30 seconds. Add the cheese on one half of the tortilla (if you're using fillings, this is the time you should put them as well). Fold over the other half and press it down using a spatula.

3. Cook each side for 2 minutes or until the tortilla is lightly browned. Remember to use a spatula to press down on the tortilla to help the ingredients stick while cooking.

4. Remove the tortilla from the pan and transfer it to a serving plate.

5. Spritz some oil in the pan and repeat steps 2 to 4 for the remaining tortillas.

6. Let the tortillas cool down completely before slicing. Serve with your favorite dips like sour cream, guacamole, mango Pico de Gallo, or salsa.

Ravioli

Servings: 4
Ingredients
For the filling:
- 680g (or 1.5lb.) Ricotta cheese, drained

- 115g (or ¼lb.) prosciutto or salami, finely chopped

- 1 cup grated Romano cheese

- 2 large eggs, slightly beaten

- 1 dash of nutmeg

- Salt and pepper, to taste

For the ravioli:
- 3 cups all-purpose flour and add more for dusting

- 4 large eggs

- 2 tbsp. olive oil

- 1 ½ tsp. sea salt

To serve:
- Sauce of your choice

- Grated cheese

Instructions

For the filling:

Add all ingredients to a mixing bowl until smooth, then set aside.

For the ravioli:

1. Add the flour and salt to a large bowl. Mix thoroughly.

2. Form a well at the center of the flour mix. Add three eggs and break the yolks using a fork, beating them lightly. Pour in the

olive oil and mix everything to make the dough. Knead for about 5 minutes until you form a smooth ball. Leave the dough inside the bowl, covering it with plastic wrap. Allow it to rest for about 20-30 minutes.

3. Cut the dough in half and place it on a floured surface. Roll each half into a 1/8-inch thick sheet using a rolling pin or pasta maker.

4. Cut out circles or squares using a cookie cutter. Make sure you cut out the same number of pieces from each sheet.

5. Put the remaining egg in a small bowl and whisk.

6. Put one teaspoon of filling in the center of each circle or square. Lightly brush the edges with the egg wash, then place the second circle or square on top of the first. Seal the edges by pressing with a fork. Do this step with the remaining pasta dough.

7. Let the ravioli rest for about an hour to dry.

8. Boil water in a large pot. Add the ravioli and cook for about 2 to 3 minutes. They are cooked once they float. Remove them using a large, slotted spoon and drain well.

9. Place the cooked ravioli on a serving plate. Toss with your favorite sauce and top with grated cheese before serving.

Hotdog Sandwich

Servings: 4

Ingredients

- 4 pieces of all-beef hotdogs

- 4 hotdog buns

- 2 tbsp. oil or unsalted butter

- ½ cup shredded cheddar cheese

- 8 pieces of lettuce leaves, optional

- Ketchup

- Yellow mustard

- Mayonnaise

Instructions

1. With just enough water to cover its bottom, heat the skillet over medium heat.

2. Add the hotdogs and allow them to cook until the water has completely evaporated. Roll them around as you go to cook all sides evenly.

3. Once the water evaporates, add the oil or butter. Fry the hotdogs for a minute or two and transfer them to a plate. Lightly toast the buns and turn off the heat once done.

4. Assemble the sandwich and serve.

Air Fryer Chicken Tenders

Servings: 4

Ingredients

- 450g (or 1 lb.) chicken tenders
- ½ cup all-purpose flour
- ½ cup breadcrumbs
- ¼ cup Panko
- 2 large eggs
- ½ tsp. garlic powder
- ½ tsp. seasoned salt
- ¼ tsp. ground black pepper

Instructions

1. Preheat the air fryer to 370°F. While at it, clean and trim the chicken tenders if necessary.

2. Mix the breadcrumbs, Panko, and seasonings in a shallow dish or plate.

3. Whisk the eggs in another bowl or shallow dish.

4. Add the flour to yet another shallow dish or plate.

5. Consecutively dip one chicken tender into the flour, eggs, and breadcrumb mixture. Make sure to coat all sides evenly.

6. Place on a plate or tray and set aside. Repeat the coating process for the remaining tenders.

7. Air fry the tenders for about 8 to 10 minutes or until golden. The air fryer size will determine if you must work in batches.

8. Serve with ketchup, ranch dressing, or honey mustard sauce.

HOW TO SHOP FOR GROCERIES

It must have been fun shopping with your parents. You get to ask them to buy the chocolates, candies, and other snacks you want. But it's an entirely different experience when you're left to buy the kitchen ingredients while following a strict budget.

Shopping for groceries is both fun and educational. It offers many learning opportunities, such as

- Identifying different food groups
- Practicing reading and writing
- Using and budgeting money
- Planning meals
- Learning more about health and nutrition

Again, we have to emphasize that you are still in the learning process. There's no need to be overly fussy at this time. You will make mistakes, and that's okay. What's important is your willingness to learn and get better.

Here are the following activities to introduce you to the basics of grocery shopping. If needed, you can enlist your parents or guardians' help.

Activity #1: Create a Meal Plan

This activity refers to how you can make your grocery list. If your household already has an existing meal plan, then all the better. You can use it as a reference. Feel free to design your meal plan if you don't have one. A one- or three-day meal plan is enough for starters. Don't hesitate to ask for your parents' assistance when needed.

Activity #2: Creating Your Grocery List

Once you have an idea of what you will be cooking, you can create a checklist of items you need in your pantry. To make a list final, you must check whether you still have the items on hand. If you still have them, are they enough until your next grocery trip? Ask your mother or father for guidance in deciding how much or how many you need to obtain.

Complete your grocery list and consider how you will categorize the items. For example, put the list of all herbs and spices together in one column. This way, you can get them all in one trip to that specific section of the grocery store. You will save time and effort in the process.

This activity will teach you about planning and familiarizing yourself with label information on the goods you use often.

Activity #3: Estimating the Budget

Once you have finalized the grocery list, write down the estimated price for each item. You may need the assistance of your parents, or you can use old receipts as references. Add everything up to get the total amount you need. Don't worry about the exact price; you only need an estimation.

Activity #4: Shopping

Take this opportunity to observe various packaging labels as well as the quality and freshness of produce. For one, learn about nutritional labels and ingredient lists, as these can affect your health. The same is true for the quality of the fresh produce you consume.

With your parent's guidance, study how one item can be of better value than another. For instance, notice how product A is a better product than product B, even though it's not a well-known brand, or how organic vegetables are healthier than conventionally grown ones.

Activity #5: Checking the Estimate vs. Actual

Were you able to buy everything on the list? Did you miss a couple of items or include something that wasn't originally on the list?

Review the receipts and check whether your purchase exceeds your estimated budget. If it does, don't despair! Prices go up all the time. But if it's about the extra chips or your favorite chocolate bar, don't beat yourself up too much. It's not like the money you used to buy them was wasted for nothing.

HOW TO STORE FOODS PROPERLY

Properly stored foods remain safe. They also retain their nutrients, flavor, and overall quality much longer.

In general, you must store foods in appropriate containers for a suitable duration. They should also be held at the right temperature. Proper food storage lessens the risk of food waste and food poisoning.

These time-tested methods will help you achieve your goal of storing and securing food well:

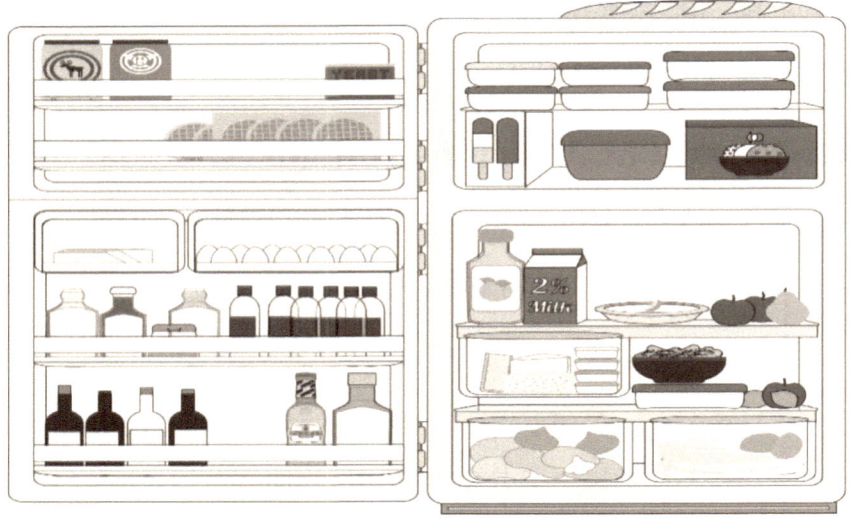

Storing in the Fridge and Freezer

You can store meats, vegetables, fresh herbs, cheeses, and leftovers in the refrigerator and freezer. Here are some guidelines on how to keep these food items properly:

- Always keep your refrigerator below 40°F or 4.5°C. Don't keep the door open for long when you get items since it can affect the temperature inside. Keeping the door open causes the cold air to escape and increases the temperature. As a result, the fridge's compressor must work hard to restore the temperature to normal. It also means an increase in your electricity bill.

- Store all your foods in covered containers or sealed bags. It will help prevent moisture loss and odor absorption.

- Store perishable foods as soon as you can. You shouldn't leave them at room temperature for over two hours.

- Never overload your refrigerator. You need the cold air to circulate inside to avoid spoilage.

- Clean your fridge at least once a week. Throw away suspicious food items even if they don't smell. Putting date labels on containers greatly helps, so make it a habit.

- Put moldy food inside a bag or wrapper. This way, mold spores will not spread everywhere. Make sure to clean the food container, pantry, or refrigerator thoroughly to remove the remaining spores. Molds spread fast on fruits and veggies, so don't forget to check on them.

Storing Fish, Meat, and Poultry

- Keep raw meat, poultry, and fish in a separate container. Place this container at the bottom of your fridge to avoid cross-contamination. Besides, the lowest shelf is the coldest part of the fridge.

- Throw away any fish, meat, or poultry that smells weird and is slimy or sticky. Discard them if you see any discoloration as well.

Storing Eggs

- Refrigerate eggs at 40°F (or 4.5°C) or lower. Storing eggs in their original carton keeps them away from strong-smelling foods. Store them at the back part since the temperature there tends to be more consistent than near the door.

- Keep raw eggs removed from their shells in an airtight container. Cover whole boiled eggs without shells with water inside a container to keep them from drying. Drain the water before using.

Storing Fruits and Vegetables

- Immediately refrigerate perishable produce, such as herbs, berries, greens, and mushrooms. Don't wash fresh produce until you're ready to use them. When ready for use, clean them thoroughly under running water and dry them with paper towels. Don't wash fresh produce labeled "ready to eat" or "pre-washed."

- Store any peeled, cut, and cooked vegetables and fruits inside a container before putting them inside the fridge.

- Keep fruits and vegetables in crisper bins in the fridge. Store fruits in a separate crisper since they release ethylene gas. This kind of gas causes vegetables to spoil quickly.

Storing Dairy Products

- Refrigerate dairy products immediately. Cover them well to avoid picking up strong odors. Place them in the back of the refrigerator where the temperature is much cooler.

- Never return the poured milk to its original container. Likewise, don't drink directly from the milk container and return it inside the fridge. Remember that contaminated milk can cause spoilage and food poisoning.

Storing Canned Foods and Grains

Store whole-grain flour and meals in airtight containers and place them on a cool, dry pantry shelf. They could last for one to three months. Alternatively, you can freeze them for about two to six months.

You can refrigerate canned food but transfer them to a covered container before doing so.

Storing Leftovers

- Refrigerate leftovers immediately, even while still warm. They shouldn't be left out of refrigeration for over two hours.

- Throw away leftovers after four days.

- If you have large amounts of leftovers, divide them between shallow containers so they cool quickly.

- Don't store leftovers in the back of the fridge. Please put them in front where you can immediately see them.

Moreover, put date labels so you will not forget their expiry date.

HOW TO RECOGNIZE SPOILED FOODS

As much as we hate food going to waste, hanging on to leftovers can be a health risk. Foods past their expiration date can cause food poisoning or illness.

Here are some reliable ways to identify if a food is already unfit for eating:

It is Slimy

If leftover roasts or deli meat have a sheen film or feel weird, toss them out. It also applies to raw meat and vegetables, especially in a salad.

When There is Mold

Mold is one of the primary signs that your food is already spoiled. It starts with tiny spores that spread quickly in food after they have passed their prime. You can see molds commonly in bread, vegetables, fruits, and dairy products. However, they also grow in locations not easily noticed (e.g., the bottom of containers or jars).

When There is Discoloration

The color change isn't always a sign of spoilage—aging food changes color sometimes without affecting its flavor and quality. If you notice slime and a change in texture, discard the food immediately.

It Smells Funny

Spoiled milk, veggies, fruit, and meat give off a sickening, foul odor. If the food smells bad, don't eat it—simple as that.

The Texture Isn't the Same

Fruits and vegetables that turn mushy and sunken are ready to be tossed out. However, remember that you can still use browned and softened apples, bananas, and other fruits in baking.

Changes in texture can also be seen in meat, fish, and dairy products.

So, when in doubt, throw it away!

HOUSE CLEANING SKILLS YOU MUST LEARN

Housecleaning is an important life skill kids need to learn. As you will live independently from your parents later when you go to college, it is a must to learn basic household tasks. We have prepared this guide to make housecleaning easy and fun for you. Let's start with your room.

Things you need to prepare:

- Cleaning cloths
- Gentle cleanser
- Dust mop
- Small bucket with water
- Sponges
- Feather duster
- Vacuum cleaner

To make these tasks fun and enjoyable, listen to music, podcasts, or an audiobook, as time can quickly pass if you enjoy it.

How to Clean Your Room

1. Prepare your cleaning tools. Start with music to make it fun.

2. Make your bed. Take out dirty linens and replace them with new ones.

3. Clean up clothes. Take dirty clothes to the laundry room and keep clean ones in your closet.

4. Organize your closet according to categories.

5. Pick up toys and put them on your shelves or organizers.

6. Free your room of trash. Return things to where they should be.

7. Wipe clean all surfaces

8. Vacuum or sweep the floor.

How to Clean the Living Room

Directions:

1. Clear out all clutter. Toys, books, dishes, magazines, clothes, etc., must be returned to their proper places.

2. Dust down the ceiling and walls. Wash with water and detergent areas that need spot wash. Include doorknobs, doors, etc.

3. Carefully dust framed art and photographs. Don't use water to avoid damaging pictures. You may use a wet cloth to wipe frames and glass.

4. Dust and clean out chairs. Make sure there's nothing that hides in corners and edges. Change the couch and throw pillow covers.

5. Clean bookshelves and all surfaces.

6. Clean the floor, including carpets and rugs, using a vacuum cleaner.

7. Clean doormats with soap and water.

How to Clean the Bathroom

Because the bathroom is usually wet, it is prone to bacteria, fungus, mildew, and unwanted odors. It's best to clean your bathroom space at least every two weeks to prevent their buildup. However, it would be best if you cleaned sinks, toilets, and other most-used areas every week. Other things you can do daily are:

1. Wipe spills and splatters on the mirror

2. Keep counter tops and sink dry

3. Clean toilet seat and faucet handles

Here are tips and tricks on how to clean the bathroom.

Tile Grout

Directions:

1. Wear rubber gloves.

2. You can use a bath cleaner or prepare a mixture of 3/4 cup of household chlorine bleach and one gallon of water.

3. Use a stiff brush when applying the formula. Apply it to a tiny area and avoid spilling or splattering the liquid on you or unsafe areas.

4. Let it sit for a few minutes before scrubbing the area. Rise with water.

Sink

Your sink can harbor tons of bacteria and viruses. Here's the best way to keep it safe from all those harmful microorganisms.

Directions:

1. Spray your sink, including faucets and handles, with disinfectants like Lysol or Clorox.

2. Allow them to remain wet for a minute or so to kill germs and other undesirable organisms.

3. Wipe with a sponge or cloth.

Toilet

Who would want to sit on a grimy toilet bowl? Despite efforts to keep plumbing flowing, you can never tell when a problem arises. It helps to know how to unclog a toilet when it happens. Learning how to deal with a clogged may not be glamorous, but the earlier you learn it, the better.

To make it sparkling clean and fresh, follow these steps.

1. Apply a generous amount of Lysol or other cleaner and leave it for about 5-10 minutes.

2. Scrub it with a stiff-bristled toilet brush and flush.

3. If the toilet is clogged, do not keep on flushing to avoid overflowing. Instead, immediately shut off the toilet's water supply and follow these directions.

4. Place the plunger over the drain and push gently on your first attempt. Trying too hard will cause the toilet bowl content to

splatter all over the place. However, the next few plunges can be more vigorous to loosen up what causes the clog.

5. Repeat until the water starts to drain up. You will need enough patience as this may take some time.

6. Wipe the toilet seat and handle with disinfectant wipes or a cloth dampened with Clorox.

7. After using the brush, remember to clean and sanitize it.

8. Clean up the toilet area.

Bathroom Tub

Directions:

1. Disinfect tub and shower areas.

2. Brush with a cleaner containing micro scrubbers and foaming cleansers.

3. Wipe away soap scum.

4. Wet the sponge and squeeze it to activate the foam.

Bathroom Floor

1. Spray bathroom floors with a multi-purpose sanitizing cleaner that won't discolor the tiles.
2. Clean with mops, rinse, and dry.

How to Clean the Kitchen

The kitchen is where adults prepare your meals. It must be kept clean at all times to ensure sanitation. Knowing how to maintain the cleanliness of your kitchen is vital to everyone's health. Here are the scheduled tasks you need to know and how to do them.

Daily Kitchen Cleaning Tasks

Depending on how you divide house chores, the overall daily schedule for cleaning must be like this:

1. Washing the dishes. Load your dishwasher and turn it on. You must handwash sharp objects and wooden utensils.
2. Clean the sink.
3. Wipe all surfaces and small kitchen appliances. People are fond of leaving anything on kitchen counters and other surfaces like the top of the fridge. Clear countertops and other surfaces of dust, crumbs, and other food debris that may cause rodents or bugs to invade your home. Take away all clutter and leave them clean.

4. Take out the garbage. You must take your rubbish out of the kitchen daily and place another clean trash bag in your garbage bin.

5. Sweep the floor. Sweep visible areas and hidden ones like underneath the table and corners.

Weekly Kitchen Cleaning Tasks

- Cleaning organizers and kitchen cabinets or cupboards
- Wiping down the inside of the microwave and stove
- Sweeping, mopping, and drying the floors

Monthly Kitchen Cleaning Tasks

- **Cleaning the oven.** Some ovens have self-cleaning features, but monthly cleaning keeps the buildup from getting out of hand if your oven doesn't have this feature.

- **Cleaning the refrigerator.** Germs can accumulate even in the fridge, especially when you miss taking our leftovers. Cleaning your fridge every month allows you to check what needs to be thrown away. Clean it using baking soda and dampen a cloth to prevent odor.

Learning different cleaning skills and organizing your home can do much to keep you and your family healthy and safe from many diseases. It may not be easy for you but remember that these are essential skills as you grow. The earlier you learn them, the better.

CHAPTER 3

SAFETY SKILLS AT HOME AND ON THE ROAD

"Safety saves sickness, suffering, sadness."
– Safety saying, circa early 1900s

As everyone is prone to minor accidents, learning some safety skills to help you avoid pain and misery caused by injuries is essential. There's nothing more effective than listening and following safety rules.

Risks are everywhere. You may encounter them in school, at home, or on the road. You must be aware of these risks, and learning to avoid or handle them can save a life, even your own. Time is also an essential factor when talking about safety and preventive measures. So, before anything wrong can happen to you or anyone you know, let's get started.

FIRST AID KIT

Even at home, you need supplies and materials for an emergency. The most essential of these is the first-aid kid. Every house must have one, for you can never tell what will happen at any time.

You must remember to label your first-aid kit and include emergency telephone numbers and a first-aid manual.

How to Assemble a First-Aid Kit

Assembling a first-aid kit is easy. You may ask your parents to buy all the things you need. You will also need the help of your parents to put everything together as you are familiar with some medicines. Ask them to explain what they are because you must know how to use them when they are not home.

Your home is one place where you feel comfortable and safe. It is essential to keep yourself safe, especially when your parents are not around. We have prepared a guide to help you stay safe by minimizing the risks of being harmed.

Choosing a Suitable Container

The first thing you do before you rush out to buy supplies and medicines you have to think of a suitable container to lodge those medical supplies. Handy as it is, your container must be durable and should have a lock for safety to prevent smaller kids or siblings from playing with its contents, as some of these are unsafe to swallow or taste.

The first-aid kit must cover the essential medical supplies you can use when you or someone is harmed. It must include a manual you should read to know what to do in case someone is bruised, burnt, cut, or fallen. If you don't know something, you may ask your parents or any adult to guide you.

In addition to the medical supplies below, your home kit must include the following.

- acetaminophen (relieves fever and pain)
- ibuprofen (eases mild to moderate pain)
- aspirin (pain reliever)
- anti-itch medicine (for mosquito bites and itching)
- calamine lotion (relieves pain, itching, and skin irritation discomfort)
- hydrocortisone (for mild inflammation)
- electrolyte solution (for hydration)

- antibiotic cream (to prevent and treat mild skin infections)
- saline wash (flush out allergen from nasal passages)

Supplies

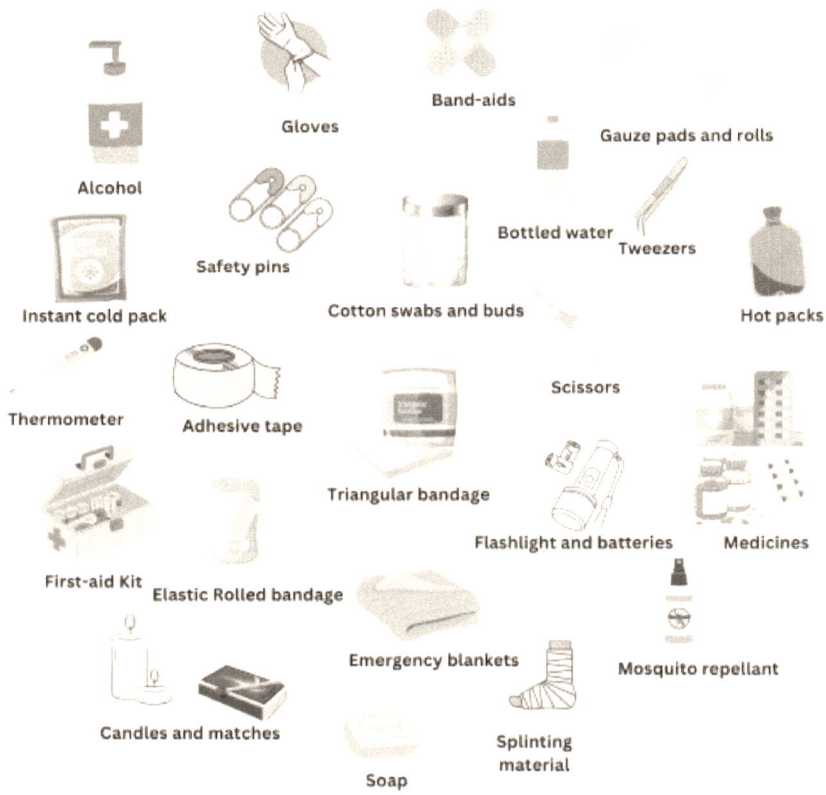

HOW TO USE 911 EMERGENCY NUMBERS

When to Call 911

You can call 911 when an emergency arises. Emergencies are scary situations for kids, but you have to understand that you can dial 911 when:

- You are lost and need help

- There is a car accident

- Someone is very sick, has trouble breathing, or can't speak, and there's no adult around to help

- The house or building is on fire

- Someone is trying to hurt you

- You hear or see someone trying to break into the house, and you're alone

- When someone passes out or when someone is sleeping and does not wake up for an extended period

- You smell or see a fire

- You are unsure if it's a real emergency, but no one is around to ask

When not to Call 911

Do not call 911 when:

- You want to ask for directions

- Your pet is injured, lost, or sick

- You're bored and need someone to talk

- You want to call out of curiosity

- You want to send a prank call, as it is a crime to treat 911 as a joke

If you call 911, be ready to answer these questions.

- What is your name?

- Why are you calling? What is the emergency?

- Where are you right now?

- What is your telephone number?

HOW TO TREAT BURNS

Common Causes of Burns

- The most common cause of burns are the following:
- abuse
- fire
- hot liquid
- hot steam
- electricity
- hot metal, glass, or other hot objects
- too much exposure to sunlight
- strong chemicals like lye, acid, gasoline, and thinner

Types of Burns

Children are at risk for burns by accident. They are prone to burn injuries from boiled water spills. They are also more likely to play with fire through lighter, matches, candles, and fireworks.

Burns are classified depending on how serious they are.

- First-degree burns are mild, like sunburns. Your skin may run red and painful, but no blisters.
- Second-degree burns are redness, swelling, blistering, and pain.
- Third-degree burns are the most serious of all types of burns. It damages not only all layers of your skin but also the nerve endings. Your skin is black, white, or red.

What You can do to Treat Burns

In cases of burns, you may call 911:

- When the burn covers 10% or more of the body
- When caused by strong chemicals or electric shock
- When the burn is on the face, sex organs, hands, feet, and joints

First-degree burns can be treated at home, while **second and third-degree burns** need medical attention. It could be infected if the burn is reddish, swollen, and tender. Call a doctor or visit a clinic if the burn shows signs of infection.

Steps in Handling Burns

#1 Soak the Part Which is Burned

- Immediately put it in cool (not cold) water or running water.
- Keep the injured part in water for about 5-15 minutes.

- Avoid putting ice over the damaged part.
- Removed burned clothing.
- If the person is burned due to a fire, remove the burned clothing. If it stuck to the skin, leave it and cut the clothing around it.

#2 Cover the Burn

- Use a clean cloth or nonstick gauze to cover the skin.
- If the burn is mild, apply ointment to the affected areas.
- Avoid putting butter, grease, or anything, and do not pop blisters.

#3 Reduce Pain

- Depending on the burn's seriousness, the doctor may give pain relievers.

HOW TO TREAT CUTS AND SCRAPES

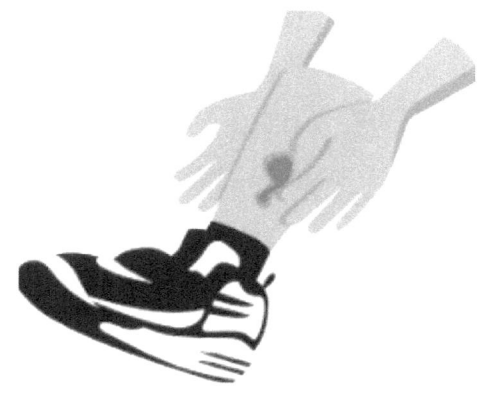

Steps to Treat Cuts and Scrapes

#1 Wash your hands before helping someone who is hurt.

#2 Firmly press the wound if it is bleeding using a clean cloth until it stops.

#3 Clean the area with running water or a clean cloth. Never use hot water. You may also use saline solution to clean the wound, but not iodine, alcohol, hydrogen peroxide, mercurochrome, or something similar. It will not clean the injury better than water but will only cause pain.

#4 If the wound is deep and dirt gets inside the skin, sanitize tweezers with boiling water or rubbing alcohol and remove it.

#5 Cover the cut or scrape with an adhesive bandage until it dries out and forms a scab. It will help protect, heal, reduce pain, and stop the wound from oozing. Use antibiotic ointment to cover the damage against infection and keep the bandage from sticking to your wounded skin.

#6 Once a scab has formed. Leave it open. But if there is a risk of irritation or dirt, keep it covered.

How to Prevent a Wound from Further Infection

To avoid infection altogether, make sure that you have your anti-tetanus shot. See your doctor if you have not had a booster shot. Generally, it is not advisable to give antibiotics to prevent the risk of infection from cuts and scrapes.

What to Do When You're Choking

Kids love to put things into their mouths, like marble, coins, and pen caps. These small items can choke a child once they slip into a child's air passage. It is dangerous and can cause death. Once the flow of air is blocked, it also cuts off the brain's oxygen supply. This condition can cause permanent damage to the child's brain.

Choking Hazards

- Any small items like popcorn, ballpen caps, marbles, and nuts
- Small parts of a child's toy
- Button batteries of watches, cameras, and electronic gadgets
- Tiny household objects such as beads, coins, buttons, etc.

Kinds of Choking

Choking signs include:

- Difficulty in breathing
- Holding their throat
- Having violent coughing
- Can't speak, cry, or cough

- Produces a high-pitch sound when breathing in

Assessing the Situation

Steps used in handling a choking incident may differ depending on the situation.

If the child can still speak and has a strong cough but has trouble breathing:

- Do not attempt to get the object from the child's mouth using your finger. You may accidentally push the object deeper into the child's throat.

- Call 911 as soon as possible, as the airway can become entirely blocked.

- Tell the child to cough. Do not attempt doing the Heimlich maneuver (See Instructions below). Coughing is a better option than the Heimlich maneuver.

- Watch closely for the object to come out and ensure that it doesn't change position and entirely block the air passage.

If the child is conscious but can't talk or make any sounds:

- Do the first two steps, but do the Heimlich maneuver this time.

- Ask someone to call 911.

- If the child stops breathing and you can't see the object, place your mouth over his mouth. Pinch the nose to shut and puff a couple of breaths into the mouth. Each breath should last two seconds.

- With the child lying on their back, do the Heimlich maneuver. Kneel by their feet. Position the heel of your hand in the middle of the child's body, between the ribs and navel. Put one hand over the other and gently but firmly apply pressure. Give 6-10 quick upward and inward thrusts.

- If the child loses their pulse, the heart stops beating. Apply CPR immediately until the child regains breathing or the paramedic arrives.

The Heimlich Maneuver

- Allow the child to stand up while holding them at the waist from the back.

- Slightly bend their body and give the child five back blows just between the shoulder blades with your free hand.

- If the object does not come out, make a fist at the child's abdomen with both hands, right above the belly button.

- With a quick motion, give the child five quick abdominal thrusts but avoid lifting the child off the floor while doing this.

- Until the child regains breathing and can cough, continue with the five sets of back blows followed by five abdominal thrusts.

HOW TO STOP A NOSEBLEED

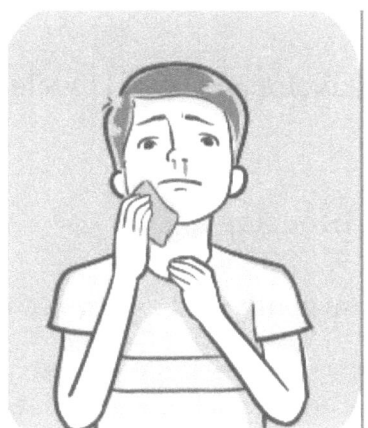

Many things cause nosebleeds in children like you. These include nose picking, getting hurt on the nose while playing, or blowing your nose too hard. If your nasal blood vessels are sensitive in hot and dry weather, you can get a nosebleed, too.

Don't freak out if you have a nosebleed while home alone. Stay calm and do the following steps:

- Gently blow your nose to remove any blood clots inside.

- Sit up and slightly lean forward to avoid swallowing your blood.

- Use your index finger and thumb to pinch your nose and breathe through your mouth. Do this for at least five minutes. Use a clock or your phone's timer to monitor the time.

- Check if the bleeding has stopped after five minutes. If it hasn't, pinch your nose shut again and wait for another ten minutes.

When the bleeding has stopped, avoid touching or blowing your nose.

To prevent nosebleeds:

- Blow your nose gently and as little as possible.

- Don't pick your nose, especially when your fingernails are long.

- Use a humidifier or steam vaporizer to prevent dry indoor air.

- Wear a head guard when playing games that might hurt your head and nose area.

- Don't go near anyone who smokes.

- Use nasal sprays or saline nose drops according to your healthcare provider's instructions.

- Don't use naproxen or ibuprofen for up to 48 hours after nosebleeds unless your doctor advises.

When should you ask for help?

Call 911 or your country's emergency hotline number when:

- Your nose can't stop the nosebleed after applying pressure for 15 minutes.
- Your nose bleeds again.
- You have a head or facial injury.
- There is a large amount of blood, even after applying pressure.
- You feel weak, dizzy, nauseous, or have difficulty breathing.

HOW TO TREAT INSECT BITES AND STINGS

Insects are everywhere, and getting bitten by one is quite common. Regardless, if the culprit is a mosquito, ant, or bee, a bite or sting can be an unpleasant experience. It may elevate to an emergency if you have an allergic reaction to bites or stings.

Reactions may vary from one individual to another. Some don't even have any. They depend on several factors:

- location of the bite or sting
- presence of irritants or toxins
- amount of toxins or irritants injected
- degree of your reaction

Symptoms

Here are the different reactions from insect bites and stings, varying in their severity:

Small Local Reaction	Pain and discomfort Itchiness Warmth and redness in the bite or sting location Swelling is less than 2 inches
Large Local Reaction	Pain and discomfort Exaggerated redness and swelling Swelling slowly enlarges over 48 hours Swelling is about 5 inches

Severe Local Reaction	Dizziness and nausea
	Fever
	Diarrhea and stomach cramps
	Swelling of face, tongue, and throat
	Difficulty in breathing
	Rashes or hives
	Enlarged lymph nodes

Preventing Insect Bites and Stings

You can reduce the likelihood of getting stung or bitten by following these steps:

- Wear shoes or sandals. Avoid going barefoot on grass.
- Avoid areas where there are beehives, wasp nests, ant colonies, such as trash bins. Avoid playing near marshes or swamps where mosquitoes usually live.
- Apply mosquito or insect repellent if you're staying outdoors.

- Don't wear dark clothing when outdoors. Choose light-colored or white clothing instead.

- Avoid using strong-smelling cologne or perfume, hairsprays, and lotions. Use unscented deodorant.

- Use a mosquito net, especially when sleeping outdoors or when you sleep with an open window.

Tightly cover trash cans and tie up garbage bags securely.

Treatment for Bites or Stings

In case you were stung or bitten, apply the following first-aid methods:

Ants 	• Clean the affected area thoroughly with soap and warm water. • Apply hydrocortisone cream. • Apply an ice compress to reduce pain and irritation. • Don't scratch the bitten area. • If a blister forms, don't pop it up. It may lead to infection. If it ruptures, keep it clean and apply antibiotic ointment. Cover it with a bandage.

Bees and Wasps 	• Remove the stinger by scraping it with gauze, your fingernail, or a credit card. Don't use tweezers or pinch it with your fingers since it may release more venom. • Clean the area thoroughly with soap and warm water. • Apply hydrocortisone cream. • Apply an ice compress if needed. • Seek emergency care if you have any allergic reactions.
Mosquitoes 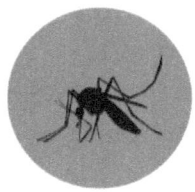	• Clean with soap and water ASAP. • Apply hydrocortisone ointment or cream to lessen itching and irritation. You can also try topical or oral antihistamines. • Never scratch the bitten area since it may lead to infection. • If you accidentally scratched it, clean the area, and apply an antibiotic cream. Cover it with a bandage if needed.

Spiders	• Wash with soap and water. • Apply antibiotic ointment or cream. • Apply an ice compress to reduce swelling. • Use acetaminophen or ibuprofen if in pain. • Use antihistamine for itching. • If you believe it is a black widow or a brown recluse, go to the emergency immediately. • Seek immediate help if you experience infection symptoms, such as nausea, stomach cramping, or pus or blister formation near the bitten area.
Jellyfish	• Rinse the stung area with vinegar or hot water for about 30 seconds. • Use tweezers to remove the remaining tentacles. • Soak the area in hot water for 20 minutes or more. • Use acetaminophen or ibuprofen to relieve pain.

	<ul><li>Don't rub the tentacles with your fingernails, towel, or anything.</li><li>Don't use an ice compress or cold water to rinse the stung area. Stingers will release more venom if you apply this.</li><li>Don't pee on the affected area.</li></ul>

When to Ask for Help

Contact 911 or your local emergency hotline if:

- A bee or wasp has stung you on the face, mouth, and neck.

- Bees, wasps, yellow jackets, or hornets have bitten or stung you over ten times.

- You experience a severe allergic reaction within two hours after getting bitten or stung. You will experience swollen face, tongue, and lips during this time.

- You will have difficulty breathing and swallowing. These symptoms may also include breaking out in hives or feeling severe itchiness.

- You feel dizzy or have lost consciousness.

HOW TO PERFORM HANDS-ONLY CPR

Many people on the verge of dying were saved through cardiopulmonary resuscitation (CPR). This technique focuses on keeping the blood and oxygen of a person when their heart and breathing have stopped.

The steps of CPR vary slightly according to whether a person is an infant, child, or adult. The main distinction is whether you perform chest compression with the following:

- Two hands for adults

- One hand for children

- One thumb or two fingers for infants

There are two types of CPR—hands-only and traditional CPR with breaths. People with no training should use hands-only CPR only. Additionally, they can only perform this technique if the distressed person is a teenager or an adult. They can't perform it on infants and children. Having said this, we will focus on the first type, which is hands-only CPR.

You may ask, "Why should I learn this skill?" One reason is for self-improvement, and the second is to be prepared for emergencies.

The thing about emergencies is that they happen when we least expect them. Knowing how to face them gives us an edge. In this case, we gain the chance to save a life. For instance, CPR on someone experiencing a cardiac arrest within the first few minutes can keep them alive until medical professionals arrive.

Follow these steps to perform hands-only CPR for teens and adults:

Assess the Scene 	• Survey the scene and ensure it's safe to go to the person needing help.
Check for Responsiveness	• Tap the person's shoulder. • Ask them if they're okay in a loud voice.

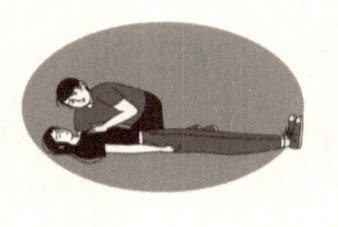	• Call 911 or your country's emergency hotline if the person is unresponsive. • If you're alone and believe the person has drowned, start CPR for 2 minutes before calling the emergency hotline.
Place in a Safe Place 	• Prepare for chest compressions by placing the person on a firm, flat surface. • Kneel beside them.
Place Hand Position 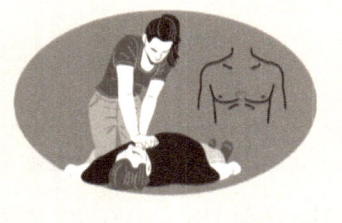	• Put the heel of one of your hands in the center of the person's chest. It is the spot between the nipples. • Lay your other hand on top of the first. • Interlock your fingers and raise them. Make sure that

	only the heel of your other hand remains on the chest.
Start the Compressions	• Use your upper body to push down on the person's chest at least 2 inches. • Perform 100 to 120 compressions per minute. • Allow their chest to draw back between compressions.
Repeat Compressions	• Continue to compress until the person begins to breathe again or help arrives. • If the person starts to breathe, help them lie on their side until medical professionals come.

SAFETY TIPS WHEN YOU'RE HOME ALONE

Things will run more smoothly and safely if you have a system. It is especially beneficial when you're at home without your parents around for instant guidance.

Below are some ideas to help you get to know the drill should you be left home alone in any case:

- Create a list that includes emergency hotline numbers, neighbors' numbers, parents' numbers, and the contact information of trusted persons nearby.

- Create an emergency plan with your parents. Practice what to do in a fire, earthquake, injury, or other emergency.

- Identify where basic disaster supplies (e.g., flashlights, batteries, first aid kit, whistles, etc.) are kept.

- Lock the doors and secure the windows, especially at night.

- Never open the door to strangers. Always double-check who is knocking or ringing the doorbell before opening the door. Peek through the peephole or window first.

- Don't open the door for salespersons or couriers. Ask them to leave the package at the door or come back at another time if they insist they need somebody to sign the papers.

- Never tell anybody that your parents aren't at home. Make excuses like, "They're busy right now. May I take the message instead?"

- Never share that you're home alone on social media.

- Don't go outside to check out a strange noise. If it worries you, call your parents, trusted neighbors, or the police.

- If there is a fire, go outside and ask help from a neighbor to call the fire department.

- Don't ask friends over when your parents aren't home unless they give the "go" signal. Never let anyone who drinks alcohol or uses drugs inside, even if you know them.

ROAD SAFETY RULES FOR KIDS

Unlike adults, kids are unaware of what to do when walking down the street. Without adult supervision and knowledge of road safety rules, you can be in danger. The National Highway Traffic Safety Administration reported that about 3% of those killed in car accidents were children. Statistics also show that about 480 kids are injured in traffic accidents daily. More disturbing is that 207 of the 4,884 pedestrians killed in traffic accidents were children. It is important to not make any compromises regarding your safety, so you should learn about road safety as soon as possible.

Here are the basics of road safety:

Know your signals. Green means GO! Vehicles move forward only when the signal turns GREEN. When the signal light turns red, all cars must come to a complete stop.

When the traffic signal turns YELLOW, cars should slow down and prepare to stop. There are times, however, that some vehicles will ignore the signal light, so stay alert at all times.

At intersections, the WALK or a walking man symbol is for pedestrians. Only cross the street if the sign turns GREEN. Check to your left and right to ensure there are no approaching cars. Cross the street only if the signal turns RED or displays the walking man.

Stop, Look, and Cross. Sometimes, a hand symbol is used. There are other symbols for pedestrians, so make sure to stay informed.

Always look for traffic signals and cross the street using a pedestrian crossing. In the absence of such markings, you should do the following:

Look to your right, then to your left, and back to your right to see if any approaching vehicles. If so, wait for the car to pass before crossing the street.

Never cross at curves, and crossing between stationary or parked vehicles is never a good idea.

Pay Attention and Listen. You may only sometimes be able to see an approaching vehicle, mainly if they are near a bend. Hence, you should listen to determine if a vehicle is approaching. Vehicles on the road frequently would signal to indicate their approach to bends and unmanned intersections.

If you hear a horn, you should halt and look to see if any vehicles are approaching. Listen for engine sounds in the area to see if there is a moving vehicle; a loud noise indicates a nearby car, and a faint sound suggests a vehicle that is far away. The sound of tires also indicates the presence of a vehicle.

Don't Run on Roads. While you might feel impatient and prefer to run across the street to the other side, refrain from doing so. While playing, you may sometimes run towards the road, but refrain from running across or along the road no matter what happens. Always remain calm on the road and never run or sprint.

Always Use Sidewalks. Stay on the sidewalk. Whether the street is busy or not, when walking alone, walk on the sidewalk to keep yourself safe on the road. However, if there are no sidewalks, keep walking on the left side, facing oncoming traffic.

Crossroads and Pedestrian Crossing. Running vehicles do not slow down unless there is a signal light, a sign, or a crossroads, which can be dangerous, so only cross at intersections and use the pedestrian crossing. You should follow the above rules if you live in a small neighborhood with no crossroads or marked junctions.

In some schools, pedestrian safety lessons are essential and are included in the school curriculum.

Never Stick Hands Outside the Vehicle. Even when the school bus is moving, there is a chance you may even stick your arm out to wave your classmates goodbye or even your head out while waving back. It is common for students to take the school bus. Sticking your hands or head out of the moving school bus or any vehicle can be extremely dangerous. If you are not cautious, you may be hit by cars approaching from the opposite direction or by objects close to the road, such as signs and trees.

Never Cross a Road at Bends. For motorists, bends are blind spots. When you cross at a bend, the vehicle drivers do not have enough time to spot you and stop, so crossing at a bend increases your chances of getting hurt.

Be Visible to Stay Safe

- When walking or biking at night, wear light-colored clothing or reflective material.

- When going out for a nighttime walk, wearing all black or blue may be a bad idea. If you want to stay safe, vehicle drivers must see you.

- During the day, dress brightly.

- Wear lights or flashing lights to make yourself visible to motorists at night.

- If you want to alert an approaching vehicle to your presence, wave your hand.

Don't Rush! You might become overly excited and rush to get somewhere or meet someone. That can be hazardous. Always remember that:

- It is dangerous to rush when getting into or out of a vehicle.

- Avoid being distracted or dragging your parent or guardian in an unexpected direction, as this can catch the adult off guard.

- When walking down the street, keep your cool and don't rush.

- Open the car doors slowly, and develop the habit of only opening the doors when your parent or guardian says so.

- Playing in the bus bay or on the roads is not permitted.

Stay Safe on a Bicycle

To stay safe while on the road, when riding your bike to school, or around the neighborhood, make sure you are aware of and follow the following cycling rules.

- When riding a bike, always wear a helmet.

- Before using the bicycle, ensure that nothing is wrong with it. Check for breaks and lights if used at night.

- Always ride in the bike lane. If there's no lane for bikes, stay on the far right side of the road (whichever is right in your country) and keep up with traffic. Keep your eyes and ears open for larger and faster vehicles approaching from behind.

- Always use light in low-visibility areas and at night to be seen by motorists. Wearing reflective material and flashing lights can help motorists notice you in the dark.

Staying Safe Inside a Moving Vehicle

- Using a car seat or seat belt, you can keep yourself safe inside a moving vehicle. To ensure that you are safe in a moving car, follow these simple rules:

- Standing inside a moving vehicle, especially a school bus or van is never a good idea.

- Students should not move around inside a school bus that is moving.

- Inside a bus, hold on to the rail for support. Wait until the vehicle completely stops before going out of it.

- Do not put any part of your body outside a moving vehicle's window.

- Always get out by the curbside.

- When exiting a car or a bus, always leave on the curbside to avoid obstructing other vehicles on the road.

If you ride the school bus every day, make sure you remember these safety precautions:

- Start early and on time to avoid having to run for the bus.

- Always fall in line when boarding and alighting from the bus.

Aside from learning about road safety rules for kids, it would be best to keep the following tips in mind to stay safe on the road:

- Fasten your seatbelts! Always wear your seat belt or be properly secured in a car seat.

- Remind your parents or guardians to use the child lock feature on the car to prevent you from opening the car doors on your own.

- Inquire with your parents about the practical application of traffic safety rules.

- Be patient, stay calm, and don't run on the road.

- Make eye contact at an intersection or crosswalk with the driver in front of you. It alerts the driver of your presence.

- Be punctual and always disciplined when crossing or walking the road.

- When crossing, avoid using cell phones or other electronic devices. Remove your headset or earphones as well.

ROAD SAFETY GAMES & ACTIVITIES

Play is an excellent way to learn important yet practical lessons. Here are some road safety activities you can learn about.

- Ask your playmate what they would do when playing on the street and the ball and the ball rolls into the middle of the road.

- Draw or paint road and traffic signs or posters to familiarize yourself.

- Crossword puzzles are fantastic learning tools for older children. Online, you can find crossword puzzles regarding road safety education for kids.

- Play a guessing game in which you make noises or sounds you will likely hear on the street and identify them.

- Use activity sheets detailing road safety. You can find road safety education worksheets on the internet for such a purpose. Automobile manufacturers, such as BMW, provide free online resources to help educate everyone about road safety.

- Make a map of roads, intersections, and symbols, and use toy cars and people to role-play safety scenes.

Road Safety Facts

Vulnerable road users such as pedestrians, stray animals, cyclists, and bikers account for roughly half of all fatalities in traffic accidents (*Road Safety*, n.d.).

Wearing a correctly fitted and high-quality helmet reduces the risk of injury and death in a crash by around forty percent (*Helmets*, n.d.).

Reduced or controlled speed can reduce the likelihood of injury during an accident (Johnston, 2004).

Compared with seat belts alone, using a car seat reduces the risks of injury in a crash by 71-82% for children. Using booster seats reduces children's risk of serious injury by 45% (*CDC*, n.d.).

Furthermore, the World Health Organization (2009) suggests that using safety belts in vehicles could reduce deaths by 45% and injuries by 50%.

Every 1 km/h reduction in speed reduces the risk of an accident by two percent (*Speed Management*, 2018).

WHAT IS ROAD SAFETY AWARENESS?

Understanding traffic rules and regulations is critical for safely walking or driving on the roads and avoiding accidents and other mishaps. Road safety awareness teaches people about traffic lights, street crossings, walkways, animal safety, speed limits, and other rules. You can ensure the safety of other pedestrians, stray animals, and motorists by learning road safety at a young age.

To cross the street safely, one must be alert and attentive, wait for the red light for vehicles and the green light for pedestrians, use the crosswalk, and never multitask or use a mobile phone.

HOW TO DEAL WITH STRANGERS

When walking home alone from school or to the bus stop, you may meet some people who want to harm kids like you, but being street smart can help you avoid these people as you can read people and handle challenging situations. Knowing how to be streetwise can keep you safe from bad strangers when you're alone or with other kids. In short, you know your way around and can't be easily lured by criminals.

Generally, strangers aren't dangerous, but some would want to hurt children, and these are the ones who are dangerous. It's not easy to tell if a stranger is out to harm you. They usually don't look mean or scary. Such people seem friendly and nice, but only because they want to lure you into abducting them. Street-smart kids can easily spot a bad guy.

Here are some safety rules that smart street kids use to follow:

Make sure your parents or any adult knows where you are. Once you step out of the house, tell anyone so they can quickly check on you.

Be with friends. Being alone with a buddy is safer while walking home or anywhere. The more companions you have, the safer you will be.

Choose safe spots. Safe spots are areas where you can access help, like police stations, restaurants, stores, family friends' houses, or fire stations. When biking or walking, be familiar with these safety spots, so you can have an escape route when in danger. Keep away from isolated places such as dark alleys and woods.

Avoid strangers asking for help. When a stranger's car suddenly pulls beside you, asking for help, be on alert. Don't come near the vehicle or put your hands near the window, as they can quickly grab you. It's nice to help, but people typically ask for help from grown-ups, not kids. If you can walk away, go to the nearest safe spot and shout for help when you feel in danger. Also, do not accept anything that a stranger offers you.

Don't easily believe a stranger. When a stranger picks you up from school telling you that your parent's asked them to pick you up because of an emergency, don't quickly believe and go with them. Your parents would have sent someone you know if this happens or would have told you if someone would come to pick you up.

Make Noise or Distraction. When in danger, make noise to attract attention. It will distract the bad guys. Shout for help so that other people can help you.

Trust Your Gut. Your gut is your second brain, and it pays to trust it, especially when you are in danger. Suppose your gut tells you that you are in trouble; believe it and act quickly. Go away as far as you can and ask any adult to call 911 if you don't have a phone.

How to Stay Safe While Riding With Strangers

Riding alone without an adult can sometimes cause harm to children, as there are reported incidents of crimes committed by drivers of taxis and other ride-sharing transport services. To ensure you're safe, consider these safety tips from the two most popular ride-sharing apps:

Think ahead. Before requesting a ride, make sure you know where to go. Check the app's safety features so you can use them in an emergency.

Stay indoors while waiting. Make your request while indoors to avoid attracting the wrong kind of attention. Avoid standing outside with your phone on hand; wait inside until you're informed that the driver has come.

Choose a spot where the driver can quickly spot you when you are crowded. When you have no option to stay indoors and in a crowded area, choose where the driver can easily pull over without blocking traffic and where you can easily be seen.

Be wise in choosing your drop-off location. Make sure to choose a well-lit busy area as it could be safer than an isolated side street. Before you enter the vehicle, confirm your drop-off location.

Don't share personal information. Never share information with any stranger, and this rule includes the driver. As much as possible, avoid talking while riding. You can never know what information you slipped off while chatting with them.

Take the back seat. When alone, choose the back seat so you can have more opportunities to take your exit when needed. It also gives you more personal space.

Remember to use your seat belt. Make sure you fasten your seat belt before the driver starts running the vehicle. Using seatbelts is required by law as a primary safety measure.

Share ride details. Ride-sharing apps have this sharing feature allowing you to share the driver's information and location. Once you're on your way, remember to share these details with your parents or family.

Be on alert during your ride. Just as you would while walking on a street, be aware of your surroundings. Pay attention to the driver and the route the driver is taking. Is the driver following the correct route? Avoid texting or having unnecessary conversations. If you feel something isn't right, speak up immediately. Over speeding, reckless driving, and making phone calls are illegal behaviors that matter most to your safety.

When in danger, call 911. Call attention through the open window or call 911 if in danger. Also, make sure that you store a number of the local police in your phone or know how to contact 911. Ride-sharing apps have a panic button on their feature for an emergency. Be sure you know how to use it before taking a ride.

How to Handle a Home Emergency

When in an emergency at home, like when someone falls down a ladder or has a stroke, you can call for help.

To make an emergency call, here's what you must do.

- Take a deep breath to relax.

- Dial 911 and tell the operator about the emergency.

- Tell them your name and exact location.

- Provide as many details as possible when giving information.

- Listen to the operator's instructions and follow them carefully.

- Stay on the phone unless the operator tells you to hang up the phone.

If the injured person is other than you and only you can help and call 911, don't rush over to the injured person after the call. Wait for the help to arrive. Moving an injured person is dangerous, primarily when a bone or neck injury occurs.

To prepare yourself and be ready to help when there's an emergency, here is what you can do.

When outside your home, ensure you are near a safe spot so you can call for help without your phone.

- Make sure that you know how to call 911 or local emergency numbers.
- If you have a cellphone, you must know how to use it in an emergency.
- Learn the basics of first-aid.

It's scary to think of emergencies, whether they involve you or any of your loved ones. But sometimes, you can't avoid an accident, and it's good to know that you are equipped and ready to handle such a situation.

Accidents can happen regardless of where you are, so it is important to know essential life skills to stay safe. Being prepared at all times is the best way to handle an emergency. And when you know what to do ahead of time, it can help you stay in control so you can help.

CHAPTER 4

HOW TO MANAGE YOUR MONEY

"The more you learn, the more you earn."
–Frank Clark

In this world, we rely on money for things we need —food, clothing, shelter, education, health care, etc. But more than money, you need to learn how to handle your money to earn more. Remember that money is not the only source of happiness. It can buy you anything but not everything. There are things more important that money can't buy, like values and character. Because money is essential, learning how to handle your money is an important skill to learn. Also included are other skills related to handling money matters like saving and shopping. It is essential to learn about these, for learning more lets you earn more.

You learn mathematics in school because it is an essential part of our everyday life, like when you go shopping. Since you go to buy something in the grocery when running errands for your mom, why not use it to improve your mathematical skill? You can practice different skills when buying things in a grocery store. Let's try some fundamental math concepts using money.

WHY YOU NEED MONEY SKILLS

"Managing money is for adults, not us!" you may argue. However, many financially responsible adults started as early as your age (with some even younger).

Besides, learning about this skill early on has its perks. It will help you:

- Understand the value of money
- Spend responsibly
- Save for long-term goals
- Become more financially literate and independent
- Have stronger abilities to manage your finances in the future

Gaining knowledge early in life, especially while still under the care of your parents, will benefit you. You can avoid costly careless mistakes that young adults usually commit because they started learning about this skill quite late.

THE VALUE OF MONEY

Understanding the value of every dollar (pound, euro, peso, etc.) you have, makes a difference. It can determine your spending and saving habits, which affect your financial stability and independence later on in life.

Kids your age already recognize which items you can buy with $1 and which you can afford with $100. You can also tell how many pennies, nickels, or dimes make $1. Since you have a good grasp of the basics, this is the perfect time to learn about wise spending and exchanges.

The following are simple methods on how to expand your learning about finances as you grow:

Learn to be Grateful	Learning how to be grateful and content is a valuable life lesson. It will teach you important things, such as: <ul><li>The real value of material things</li><li>Wants vs. needs</li><li>Responsible spending</li></ul>

Learn to Give	Well-rounded people know the value of giving. You can start by volunteering for a cause, for example, selling cookies and donating profits to the cause. You can also choose a charity or organization you want to help personally.
Learn the Value of Work	Look for simple job opportunities where you can earn extra money. This way, you will understand the equation: **Time = Money**.
Save Money	Save changes in a piggy bank or ask your parents to help you open a bank account. Saving should never be the least of your priorities. Instead, make it a part of your daily financial habits.
Avoid Impulsive Buying	Avoid buying unnecessary things right away. Consider how it will affect your budget or savings.

Learn to Weigh Priorities 	Ask yourself, "Do I really need this? Is this worth the time I spent earning the money I'm about to spend?" Perhaps buying a new video game could negatively impact your budget for the summer trip you planned with your friends.

HOW TO EARN MONEY AS A KID

Sometimes you want to buy something that costs more than what you have. How do you earn more and help you save money more quickly?

You can pursue your goal with effort, creativity, and the go-signal from your parents. Below are some ideas that will help you get started:

Do Extra at Home 	Ask your parents for extra monetary support in exchange for your effort. For example, offer them your lawn or garage cleaning services.

Extend the Offer to Your Neighbors 	Tell your neighbors that you're providing odd job services, such as tending their lawns, snow shoveling, house sitting, and cleaning.
Wash Cars 	Ask permission from your parents if you could turn your driveway into a neighborhood car wash. You can also offer home services if your clients don't have the time to drop by.
Babysit Little Kids 	Take a babysitting class if you're legally old enough. Parents are always on the lookout for reliable babysitting services.

Offer Dog-Walking or Pet Care Services 	If you love dogs and other animals, offer pet care services.
Sell Unwanted Items 	Do you have secondhand items taking up space in your room or house? Set up a garage sale or sell them online.
Sell Candies or Pastries 	Bake cookies, muffins, cupcakes, and brownies. Sell them online, in your neighborhood, or at events. Developing cooking and baking skills is one of the best ways to earn money in the future. You can profit from these skills almost immediately and in the near future.

HOW TO SPEND WISELY

Shopping and buying can be tricky, even for adults. Simply looking in a grocery or department store will lead you to believe that you need a hundred things. If you're not careful, you might find yourself buying unnecessary things.

There are effective methods to avoid impulsive buying. Here are some of them:

Always Create a List 	Having a shopping list before heading out makes a huge difference. It's a key strategy to minimize impulse buying. The shopping list will keep you in line by reminding you of your goals.
Research about the Product 	Know about the product you want to buy. For example, you need a study chair. Research it online and make product comparisons. Create a list of at least three stores where you can buy it. If purchasing online, make sure

	to check on the customer feedback. Reach out to the seller if you have further questions about the product.
Check Out Clearance Aisles	Most stores set up clearance aisles. Visit there first to check if you can buy some items on your shopping list at a discounted price.
Learn about How Marketing Strategies Work	Supermarkets strategically put expensive items on eye level while placing cheaper ones at the bottom. They offer multi-bulk offers, which can be costlier than buying them per piece. They also put items like candies and chocolates near checkout tills to encourage last-minute impulse buying.

Learn How to Save Money 	Use your creativity to save money. Ideas might be: • Cooking your own food at home instead of going out at a restaurant • Searching materials in dollar stores instead of regular retail stores. • Inviting friends for a Netflix marathon instead of going out to the movies.
Learn about Couponing 	Collect coupons from product packaging, store ads, retailer apps and websites, coupon apps or databases, and newspapers. Take advantage of loyalty programs as well.

Shop at Thrift Shops and Garage Sales 	Many people find treasures in thrift stores and garage sales. Some even buy goods from these shops and sell them online at higher prices. You can even use this buy-and-sell strategy to gain money.
Limit Your Time Eating Out 	Eating in fast food restaurants, diners, and cafes can be expensive. Why not reserve those times during occasions? Besides, homemade food is much healthier than restaurant food.
Do a Self-Check 	Ask yourself if the item you want to add to the cart is something you need or can live without.

Track Your Expenses 	List your everyday purchases and add them up by the end of the week. Compare this with the total amount of your allowance and income from your side jobs (if any). This practice can be an eye-opener and help you think about your spending habits.

HOW TO SAVE MONEY

Saving money is pretty challenging, but it is a crucial life skill. It's also a habit that you must establish at an early age.

Starting the habit can be tough, so here are a few methods that will help:

Set Your Goals 	Saving money is easier when you have a goal in mind. Let's say you want to buy a bicycle or have a budget for your pre-planned summer vacation with friends.

	Include a timeline in your goals. For example, "I will save $150 by the end of November."
Keep Your Money Safe	It doesn't matter if it's in your piggy bank, jars, or inside the closet, as long as it's somewhere safe. Don't bring your savings to school or keep everything in your wallet. Moreover, don't tell anyone where you keep your money or how much you have saved.
Use Designated Containers	Label your piggy bank, jar, or any container according to your goals. For example, designate one piggybank for "summer vacation," one for "new rubber shoes," and another for "college tuition." This method is a simple way to organize and monitor your savings.

Track What You Have Saved 	Make a chart of your savings— either manually or digitally. This way, you can easily monitor how much money you've already saved. You can also use age-appropriate saving apps, such as **GoHenry** and **Pennybox**.
Find Fun Things that Don't Cost Anything 	Look for fun activities that don't cost anything. Play badminton with your friends at the park instead of going to the movies or eating out. You can also read in the library, paint or draw, and play free online games.
Earn Your Own Money 	Earn money by doing chores at home or for your neighbors. You can also make crafts and list them online. If you have decent baking skills, use that to your advantage. There are countless ways to earn money. All you must do is be creative.

Save First Before Spending 	The first thing to do when you receive money from your parents or job is to keep a bigger portion of it as part of your savings. You can keep the lesser portion (about 10% to 20% of the money you received) for your expenses. So, if you received $10, keep the $1 to $2 for spending.
Talk Money with Your Parents 	Tell your parents about your saving goals and ask them for further guidance. If your parents know about your intention, they might give you incentives and more opportunities to earn. They will also teach you more money-saving methods and lessons you can bring to adulthood.
Don't Take Much Money When Going Out	The chances of spending more tend to be greater when you bring too much money. For example, you and your friends plan to go shopping. Bring enough money

	for things you need to buy, the transportation, for eating, and a few extra dollars just in case. If you have a change, put it away with the rest of your savings.
Don't Let Your Mistakes Discourage You 	When you're learning something new, you are bound to commit errors. So, expect that you will commit mistakes and forgive yourself for committing them— these two are part of the process. But it shouldn't end there. Learn from those mistakes so that you can do better next time.

THE DIFFERENCES BETWEEN NEEDS AND WANTS

Needs are those things necessary in our everyday life. Examples of needs include water, air, food, shelter, and clothes. Wants are things that are convenient to have, but we can still survive without having them. These include candies, roller skates, and soft drinks.

161

Can you identify needs and wants from the list below? Put **N** if the item is a need and **W** if it's a want.

Vegetables	Gown	Eggs	Swimming pool	Music box
Cookies	Marshmallows	Toy train	Video games	Fruits
Sports car	Bottle of water	House	Shoes	Toilet

Let's talk about this further. Food is something necessary for us to live. However, there are certain foods that we can live without. Take a look at this:

Foods We Need	Foods We Want

Sometimes, your needs may differ from other people depending on the situation. Therefore, the things you buy will also vary from theirs. Take a look at these two families as an example:

Anna's family prioritizes a balanced diet.

Belle's family is vegetarian. Their diet is mainly plant-based.

Let's compare each family's shopping list, which consists of the food they need and believe will make them stay healthy.

Anna's Shopping List	Belle's Shopping List
• Chicken breast	• Brussels sprouts
• Red meat	• Carrots
• Salmon	• Tomatoes
• Eggs	• Lentils
• Broccoli	• Onions
• Carrots	• Garlic
• Potatoes	• Sweet potatoes
• Onions	• Avocado
• Bananas	• Bananas
• Oranges	• Lemons
• Parsley	• Strawberries
• Chives	• Pasta
• Rice	• Tofu
• Olive Oil	• Eggs
• Vinegar	• Maple syrup

As you can see, Belle's shopping list has no meat products since her family doesn't need them in their diet.

Let me give you another scenario: A big typhoon devastated Juan's hometown. There's no electricity, tap water, and internet connection. Many houses have been destroyed, including Juan's home. Juan and his family need certain things to get by. Can you spot these things among the images below?

You're correct if you choose all of these.

People don't need these things under normal circumstances. However, Juan's situation gives us the idea that these are essential for them. This also teaches us that our needs may depend on our current situation.

Knowing the things you need versus the items you want enables you to make wise financial decisions, too. Here's the situation:

You need a new pair of running shoes but only have a limited budget since you're still saving up to buy a new computer.

Pair A	Pair B
$68	$120

Pair A is from a not-so-popular brand, but customer reviews say it's durable and comfortable. Pair B is fashionable and comfortable. It's also a product of a trendy brand. Which of the two pairs do you think suits your needs?

Understanding the difference between needs and wants will help you establish fundamental money skills. You will learn how to develop a budget and self-discipline that will lead to wise financial decisions.

SHOPPING SKILLS

Many students find it hard to learn Mathematics, but do you know that you're using math in your daily routine? You're using math when counting how much you have and how much is left of your daily allowance. You're also doing math when doing physical exercises and counting how many times you have to repeat one set.

Math Skills at Work: Grocery Shopping

Before rushing to the grocery store, you must have a list of items you will buy. Write an estimate of the cost of each item. You probably have done errands before, so you may know how much these items cost. If not, ask your mom to prepare the list for you, along with the estimated price of each item.

Addition and Subtraction

See if you have enough money to buy everything on the list. Get the total by adding up all estimated costs. After adding up everything and getting the sum, deduct it from your budget or the money handed to you for these grocery items.

Comparison

You see that you will have different choices when you are in the store. If you are old enough to make a comparison, you can get a better deal for your money by doing the actual calculation.

For example, you can choose between buying 2 pounds of grapes for $2 or 3 pounds of the same item for $3,50. You can select better by dividing the cost by quantity if both have the same quality.

Option 1: $2.00/2 = $1.00 per pound

Option 2: $3.50/3 = $1.16 per pound

It's now clear that option 1 is a better deal.

Multiplication

When you need to buy more than one item, multiply the cost of one unit by the number of pieces you need to get the total estimate.

For example, you need to buy four oranges at $1.50 each.

$1.50 x 4 = $6.00 - the cost of 4 oranges

Money

With the various bills and coins, you can practice math at home. Practicing with currency is easier to learn since you have the primary tool for buying anything. Older kids can use coupons to see if they can have a better deal using coupons.

How to Balance a Checkbook

You may have seen your parents having a checkbook. This is where they get the checks they issue for paying for things they buy. The issuing bank that maintains their checking account pays the checks they have issued. The checkbook includes a summary of bills they have paid out of their checking account, so they will know where their money goes. Later, when you have your income, you will also have your checkbook. So, the earlier you learn how to balance your checkbook, the better.

Every time you issue a check or make payments, you have to subtract it from your latest balance to update it to see your updated account balance. It will be easy to see what's left of your money in your checking account.

Start practicing this skill by taking notes of the items you have purchased from the grocery store. You can go through only some of what is in a real checkbook. What you need to practice is how to balance it. To learn, get a piece of paper. Divide it into four columns.

DATE	ITEM	AMOUNT	BALANCE
12/01/2023			$500
12/01/2023	Milk	$5	$495
12/02/2023	Apples	$10	$485
12/02/2023	Orange	$6	$379
12/02/2023	Potatoes	$9	$370

MAKING SPENDING DECISIONS

There are choices you have to make in your everyday life. While your parents make decisions for you when you're too young, you will begin making simple decisions as you grow. If you are allowed to make decisions early in life, it will be easier for you to make decisions later.

From ages 9-12, you can make choices when presented with various options. We have activities here designed to help you make choices.

These activities aim to attain the following objectives:
- To analyze the different choices
- To develop logical patterns in your behavior
- To be able to make a choice in a prepared environment
- To gain self-confidence while making your choices

Grocery Shopping Activity

Your mom asks you to check on the prices of the following items before buying them. You visit two different grocery stores, and here's what you get. Calculate the total price for all the goods if you buy them from Store A. Do the same for Store B and decide where you can get a good deal. Write your answers in the column provided.

Item	Quantity	Store A		Store B	
		Cost per Unit	Total	Cost per Unit	Total
Apples	2 lbs	$3.20/lb	$	$3.25/lb	$
Bananas	1 lb	$0.92/lb	$	$0.95/lb	$
Carrots	1 lb	$2.15/lb	$	$2.05/lb	$
Potatoes	5 lbs	$4.06/lb	$	$4.50/lb	$
Onions	1 lb	$1.37/lb	$	$1.40/lb	$
Beans	1lb	$3.93/lb	$	$3.95/lb	$
Sugar	5 lbs	$2.56/lb	$	$2.50/lb	$
Eggs	1 dozen	$4.99/doz	$	$5.15/doz	$
Milk	2 gallons	$4.98/ gal	$	$4.75/gal	$
Cooking oil	48 fl oz	$5.67/fl oz	$	$5.60/fl oz	$
TOTAL			$		$

Learning how to handle your money involves learning mathematic skills. You can learn it in school and at home or when buying what you need, and it is involved in your everyday life.

CHAPTER 5

HOW TO DEAL WITH CONFLICTS AND DIFFICULT EMOTIONS

"Conflict is inevitable, but combat is optional."
— Max Lucado

Conflict is always challenging, and some battles can't be avoided. When it happens, take time to think first before doing something about it. Take time to analyze the situation. Know where the conflict comes from and its reasons, then think of a better way to deal with it. As most conflicts are, you may settle it peaceably with the other person and don't need to fight over trivial matters.

Not all conflicts are harmful. Some are healthy and may even benefit you. Sometimes, it's not necessary to deal with conflict aggressively. Instead, work it out with the other person.

In life, we can't always please people, or we can't always please all. No matter how you do your best, others will see it differently. Because of these differences, conflicts can arise at any time, and if you spend your time and energy dealing with all disputes that come your way, everything will be wasted, including your life.

WHAT IS A CONFLICT?

A conflict is a situation where there is an expressed struggle between two or more individuals with opposing goals, needs, ideas, and desires. A conflict can arise when one person feels the presence of a threat and responds according to how they think about the situation. Because a conflict is considered a threat, it will only go away by itself if you do something to resolve it. You can't just leave a conflict alone or refuse to face it. Neglecting to resolve a conflict will only worsen it.

Factors like experiences, culture, values, and beliefs can impact your activity or behavior toward conflict. Note that not all conflicts are damaging. Conflict can also be an opportunity for growth. Once you can resolve conflict, it can build trust. So if you have a conflict with a friend or sibling, once you can address it, your relationship will grow, and you will get closer.

CAUSE OF CONFLICT IN A RELATIONSHIP

People often disagree over differences in values, ideas, perceptions, motivations, and desires that trigger conflict. These differences can appear minor and insignificant, but strong emotions can get involved because of underlying opposing needs. For example, disputes can arise between friends when both are aiming to reach the top rank in class or who is the most popular student in the school. The conflict may occur because of their need for recognition.

The needs of each individual are significant to the success of their friendship, and when there is a lack of understanding about these differing needs, it can pave the way for conflicting interests. However, if you recognize these conflicting needs and are willing to understand and find solutions without compromising the relationship, it can serve as an opportunity for growth.

MANAGING AND RESOLVING CONFLICTS

How to Respond to Conflicts

The earlier you learn to manage conflicts, the sooner you develop your emotional intelligence, which can help in conflict tolerance and prevention. There are ways to resolve a conflict peacefully. Follow these steps, and you will quickly and calmly address a problem with anyone with whom you disagree.

Step #1 – STOP before things get out of control, take a step back and calm down your emotions. Allowing anger to set in will make conflict more difficult to resolve and make matters worse than they could have been. Allow each other a few minutes to cool down. It will prevent both of you from saying or doing anything you regret later. It is essential to recognize the reason why you are angry.

Step #2 — UNDERSTAND what the conflict is all about. Most often, a fight can start with you knowing what causes it and how it started because your emotions take over your reasoning. You lose all reason when you are too angry as your emotion takes over. However, it is vital that after you have calmed down, you understand the problem so that you can express yourself well. Ensure that both of you have a clear understanding of what the disagreement is all about. Clarify what each of you wants and doesn't want. If you have done wrong, which leads to conflict, be honest and don't be afraid to recognize your fault.

Step #3 — THINK positively instead of allowing anger to take over, think of positive options and find a solution. After settling your disagreement, you still have to find a solution to address the problem. You can't leave it hanging, or it will just come back.

Speak to each other kindly and honestly and commit to whatever solution you find.

Step #4 — CHOOSE what's best for both of you. Agree on a fair solution that can meet both of your needs.

Step #5 — ASK for an apology to the other person. After accepting that you are wrong, be brave to say sorry. Asking for an apology is not shameful, and you should not hesitate to do it.

Step #6 — RESPECT others' opinions. Even if you can't agree, you must respect your decision and not go back to what you said.

Effective conflict resolution requires you to remain patient, positive, and sincere. Therefore, avoid doing any of the following:

- Using physical violence
- Name-calling
- Insulting someone's intelligence
- Interrupting the other person
- Refusing to listen

Healthy and Unhealthy Ways of Resolving Conflicts	
Healthy	**Unhealthy**
The capacity to understand and respond well to others.	The inability to recognize and respond well to others.
Having healthy reactions like being calm, trustful, and humble.	Reactions like explosive responses and feeling irritated, insulted, and harmful.
Ready to forgive and forget and not hold a grudge.	Unhealthy consequences of conflict such as rejection, loss of love, separation, fear of refusal, and embarrassment.
The ability to find the balance and not seek punishment for the other person.	Inability to find the balance and listen to others' opinions.
Believing that face-to-face confrontation is the best when settling a conflict.	Reluctant to settle conflicts and expecting a negative outcome.

The success of resolving a conflict depends mainly on your ability to:

- Manage stress quickly while staying alert and calm
- Control your emotions and behavior
- Pay attention to the feelings expressed
- Be aware of and respect differences

Communicating Effectively During a Conflict

- You need to learn and practice two core skills to resolve a conflict successfully
- Quick stress relief
- Emotional awareness

Core skill 1: Quick Stress Relief

You encounter stress daily and may even be unaware of it. Stress has its good and bad points. Once stressed, you are more focused on accomplishing something, but the destructive effects of stress often defeat the good ones. If stressed, your emotional awareness is so limited that you would not even understand your needs. You must understand your needs to communicate with others and identify your troubles.

The best and quickest way to reduce stress is by engaging in your different senses—sound, sight, smell, taste, touch—or moving. Everyone responds differently to stress, so find what soothes your senses best. Can drinking milk calm you? Other ways could be reading books, playing puzzles, or inhaling a relaxing scent.

Everyone is different, and you need to explore to discover what works best for you. You can stay calm and focused when you know how to quickly relieve yourself of stress.

One of the surefire strategies for regulating your nerves is through social interaction. Having someone caring to listen to you can quickly soothe your senses and release tension. Maintaining a network of close relationships is critical to your mental health to always have someone to lean on in times of stress.

How to Bring Your Senses to Your Rescue

Sight

- Surround yourself with colors that can lift your mood.
- Take a walk to a park, a beach, or any area where you can enjoy the beauty of nature.
- Place a vase of flowers in your room or anywhere in your home.
- Take a look at your flower garden.
- Look at a cherished memento or photo.

Touch

- Enjoy the touch of the sunlight in the early morning.

- Feel the freshness of the morning dew as it touches your bare skin.
- Play with a stress ball.
- Hold any moving object like a stuffed animal.
- Wear anything comfortable for your skin.
- Touch any object with a texture you may find relaxing.

Taste

- Savoring a treat can be relaxing, but be mindful of what you eat and indulge your sense of taste in moderation.
- Chew sugar-free gum.
- Take a small bite of dark chocolate.
- Enjoy a healthy, crunchy bite of carrots, celery, nuts, or trail mix.
- Have a refreshing cold drink, a glass of hot milk, or a steaming hot soup.
- Have a bite of your favorite fruit.

Smell

- Spray on your favorite cologne.
- Smell the aroma of brewed coffee.
- Enjoy the smell of roses and the fresh morning air.

- Light a scented candle.
- Smell the scents of different essential oils.

Movements

- Go for a walk or run.
- Dance around.
- Move your head in circles.
- Play ball with a friend.
- Do anything that involves movement.

Another way to relieve stress quickly is to take a few deep breaths. A breathing exercise is a form of meditation designed to calm your senses. To take advantage of the stress-relieving benefits of meditation, simply take a few breaths, extending your exhale. Do this for as long as you want.

One common breathing exercise is the 4-7-8 relaxation technique. To do this, you must inhale for four seconds, hold it for seven seconds, and release your breath for eight seconds. Repeat it at least three times or more.

If you have trouble finding sensory techniques that work for you, look for inspiration around you – from your memories to your insights as you go about your day.

Memories: Try thinking back and remembering what you did as a child to calm down. Do you have a favorite pillow, teddy bear, or stuffed toy that eases your emotions when hugged?

Parents: Did you notice what your mother or father did to blow off steam? Do they feel more relaxed after getting out of the house, taking a long walk, or simply getting busy with something they can put their hands into?

Watching Others: Observe how people deal with stress to know how they stay focused under pressure; for example, boxers release muscle tension before entering into a fight, and baseball players chew gum to relieve themselves of stress.

Imagination:

- Once you get used to drawing upon your sensory toolbox, imagine vivid sensations when stress attacks.
- Close your eyes.
- Imagine the warmth of your pillow on your face or the effect of a cool breeze on your skin.

These memories can have the same calming and energizing effects on your brain. The next time you experience stress, you will always have a handy quick stress relief tool.

Core skill 2: Emotional awareness is the key to understanding yourself and others.

How can you communicate effectively if you are unaware of your feelings? Effective communication is vital in resolving conflicts and disagreements.

Understanding emotions is simple, but some people try to bury deep inside strong negative emotions like sadness, fear, and anger. But if you are afraid to face such emotions, handling conflict will be challenging since the ability to handle disputes depends on how you are connected to these feelings. Once you are aware of your emotions, you can:

- Understand other people's emotions as well
- Recognize and understand what troubles you
- Find ways to control your emotions
- Clearly and effectively communicate with others
- Easily influence other people
- Become motivated to resolve conflict

CONTROL YOUR EMOTIONS AND BEHAVIOR

How to Identify Your Emotions

Emotions are part of human nature. They tell us what we are going through and have helped us react. While we are babies, we can sense our emotions, but we can't name what emotions we have at a specific time or why we have them. But as we grow older, we begin to understand more about emotions. Because we learn to identify and express them, we no longer react as kids do. We get better at identifying what we feel and why we feel them. We become more aware of our emotions.

Emotional awareness lets us know what we need and want, the same as what we don't need or don't want. Because of emotional awareness, we build better relationships by talking more clearly about what we feel, moving past difficult emotions, and avoiding or resolving conflicts.

To build emotional awareness, follow these three simple steps.

#1 —Make a daily habit of being aware of how you feel in different situations.

#2 — Rate how strong the feeling is on a scale of 1-10.

#3 — Share your feelings with people close to you.

The best way to build awareness around your emotions is to practice them. After all, there are no wrong or good feelings. It's just a matter of knowing and labeling them. Never judge your emotions!

How to Control Your Emotions

Controlling emotions is managing emotions to complete tasks, direct behavior, and achieve goals. If you are disappointed because your parents did not give in to your demand, having this ability can help you quickly recover from disappointment.

Controlling emotions is managing emotions to complete tasks, direct behavior, and achieve goals. If you are disappointed because your parents did not give in to your demand, having this ability can help you quickly recover from disappointment.

Consider the following ways to control your emotions.

- Take time to figure out your feelings and allow yourself to experience them. Identifying an emotion clears the way to feel relief from its negative impact.

- You'll need to know what you're feeling to express emotion in words. It may help you to do some breathing exercises.

- When you're confused about your negative feelings, you feel something you aren't sure what. But once you name your feelings, not only do you begin to understand what it is, but you also realize what causes it. The clarity and acceptance of emotion can help you feel better.

- Exercise. Ride your bike, skateboard, go surfing, run, or do something to help you release your pent-up energy.

- Move with your favorite movies. Dancing, headbanging, and enjoying yourself can lighten your mood.

- Do an activity to enjoy. Doing something you want, like playing a sport, making social media clips, and any fun activity will help you remember the good things and move on.

How to Control Emotions in the Classroom

- When there's something you don't understand, raise your hand to seek help from your teacher.

- When you do not do well on your test, tell yourself to study more to get good grades next time.

- When you forget to do your homework, tell yourself to check your notes as soon as you arrive home, so you will remember to do your homework.

- When you feel your heart speeding up because you don't know the answer to some questions in the exam, take a few deep breaths to relax or drive away any mental block.

Once your mind is clear of cobwebs, you will see that some questions are easy to answer.

HOW TO COMMUNICATE MORE EFFECTIVELY DURING A CONFLICT

Practical communication skills can help settle a conflict as soon as it arises. Here are some skills to help you communicate effectively during a conflict:

- Use "I" statements to explain your side.

- Avoid throwing hurtful words or displaying lousy behavior just because you're hurt.

- Discuss the problem openly and directly with the other person. As much as possible, avoid involving others.

- Listen actively to the other side. Refrain from interrupting while the other tells you their side of the story.

- Clarify what you understand from their explanation to avoid more misunderstanding.

- Learn to apologize for contributing to the dispute. Rarely does a conflict arise because of one person. It always takes two to disagree. Asking for an apology won't harm or diminish you but can pave the way for a quick settlement.

- Be kind. Kindness is the best way to stop hurting each other.

HOW TO HANDLE PEER PRESSURE

What is Peer Pressure?

Your peers are people your age, such as your classmates. When other kids attempt to get you to act a certain way or compel you to do something, it's called peer pressure.

Even if your peers aren't pressuring you, you might want to emulate them. It's understandable to want to fit in.

It's fine to do what your friends and classmates do as long as it feels right. But the most important thing is to be honest with yourself, even if that means being different from your peers.

How Do Peers Affect You?

Peers influence one another simply by spending time together. They learn from you, and you learn from them. Listening to and learning from others your age is natural.

Peers can influence you in a variety of ways. For example, you see what kids in your class are wearing at one time, like it, and wear something like that, too. It is reciprocal. Your peers may observe what you do and decide to emulate it.

Peers can have a positive influence on one another. Perhaps a student in your science class taught you a simple way to remember the solar system's planets. You may admire an athletic friend and strive to copy them. You got others interested in your new favorite book, and now everyone is reading it.

Peers, on the other hand, can negatively influence one another. They may attempt to persuade you to do something you know is wrong. What if a few kids at school try to get you to skip class with them? What if a soccer teammate tries to persuade you to be rude to another player and never pass the ball to them? What would you do? Would you cave in and succumb to peer pressure? Or would you resist peer pressure if you knew it was wrong?

It's sometimes easier to know what to do than to do it. Thinking about it ahead of time prepares you to do the right thing. You may set an excellent example for your peers when you do the right thing.

Why Do Some Kids Give In To Peer Pressure?

Some children give in to peer pressure because they want to be liked or believe it will help them fit in. Some are concerned that other children will tease them if they do not conform to the group. Others follow because they are intrigued. Perhaps they want to try something that other people are doing. They may agree if they believe "everyone else is doing it," even if they know better.

How to Say No to Peer Pressure

Understand what is right. Trust your instincts about what is right and wrong. Ask yourself, "Is it correct?" You've probably guessed the answer. It is easier to stand firm when you know what to do and when you know that you are doing what is right.

Have a trusted friend who will stand with you. It can be highly beneficial to have at least one other peer willing to say "No," as this lessens peer pressure. It's lovely to have friends who will support you when you don't want to do something against your will or that of the majority.

Choose good friends. You've probably heard a parent or teacher say, "Choose your friends wisely," One of the main reasons for this is peer pressure. If you choose friends who don't do drugs, skip class, smoke cigarettes, or lie to their parents, you will likely not do those things, even if other kids do.

Help a friend. You may have noticed that a friend is having difficulty resisting peer pressure. To help, you can say, "I'm with you — let's go."

Walk away. You can still do things if you're alone and face peer pressure. You can avoid peers who put you under pressure to do something you know is wrong. Tell them, "Nah," and walk away. It won't hurt you to lose them. Even better, find new friends and classmates to hang out with.

Seek the advice of an adult. If you're having trouble dealing with peer pressure, seek advice from an adult you can trust. Speak with a parent, a teacher, or a school counselor. It can help you feel a lot better. Furthermore, they can assist you in preparing for the next time you face peer pressure.

You can't avoid conflicts as they are a part of your life, but knowing their causes and emotions will help you handle them appropriately.

CHAPTER 6

HOW TO DEVELOP GOOD MANNERS AND SOCIAL SKILLS

"Manners are the guiding principles of respect and social interaction, and etiquette is the unwritten code of exact rules." – William Hanson

Having good manners and etiquette is important in your interaction with others. If you want to be recognized as a good kid, have lasting friendships, and be successful, it is essential to know how to conduct good manners and the correct etiquette wherever you are. Proper etiquette communicates what you are to others. Your behavior reflects the kind of character you have, and people never miss it.

Excellent and proper etiquette are appropriately conveyed in the Golden Rule, which emphasizes treating others how you want to be treated.

There may be certain situations when you can be out of your element. You may need to be made aware of the standard practices or rules. However, you can still be courteous and kind and show good manners. Manners are empathic to the feelings of others. If you have that awareness and a bit of kindness, you can have good manners and never go wrong.

THE IMPORTANCE OF GOOD MANNERS

Humans are social beings and are expected to follow specific rules of social interactions for interpersonal relationships. Social etiquette must be followed to show respect and good upbringing to everyone in a social situation. The practice of social etiquette reduces conflict and promotes harmony while influencing how others perceive you. It allows you to leave a lasting impression on other people.

What are Good Manners?

You might hear someone say that possessing good manners is old-fashioned today. Don't believe them! Good manners are fundamental to success in many areas, and their benefits impart from childhood through adulthood.

Courtesy, etiquette, and good manners are the building blocks of a healthy society. These things are not only essential, but they are tremendously beneficial and significant as we interact with each other and build relationships. Exercising good manners is one effective means of expressing respect, courtesy, and compassion.

We must practice good behavior and politeness towards others because we care about how we affect others through our actions. Because we interact with people daily, how we behave toward them often influences their responses toward us, whether these reactions are good or bad. Beyond that, good manners are crucial because they inspire others to be kind and considerate.

Why You Need Good Manners

Without manners and etiquette, the world can become a mess. The significance of practicing good manners in life cannot be overstated, but let me point out a few of its most powerful benefits.

Good Manners Instill Confidence

When you know basic social manners, you know how to act appropriately in any situation, thereby eliminating doubts and self-consciousness. It also protects you against embarrassment over any inappropriate action or misstated words.

Good manners help you become a more pleasant kid and draw others around you like a magnet. Knowing how to behave in what people expect of you in social situations will earn you positive reinforcements from peers and help you build your confidence and boost your self-esteem.

Good Manners Enhance Your Charm

Good manners and etiquette add a set of extra charm to your personality and enhance your social skills. Being aware of your manners from an early age makes them like second nature and they become a part of who you are. Learning to say simple words like "please" and "thank you" or offering your seat to a disabled person or elderly are common courtesies that create a positive impression.

Good Manners Make the Best Impression

Making the first impression is important as it sets the stage for future opportunities and relationships. When you meet a person for the first time, they have no previous knowledge about you. Naturally, they would assume you to be the person based on how you behave and carry yourself, including how you speak. It can be intimidating meeting someone for the first time, but when the person has good manners, it eases the burden. You will never know where a good first impression will take you.

Good Manners Open Doors to Opportunities

Sometimes manners can open doors that even the best education can't. Unforeseen, life-changing opportunities can be made possible, and those opportunities aren't limited to career choices.

When you are mindful of other people, they will notice your good behavior, and that impression will stick with them because it makes them feel good. So, when the opportunity comes along, they always think of you first.

Good Manners Cultivate a Heart for Others

Think of manners as . . .

- offering help to others
- holding the door for opportunities
- making eye contact when in a conversation

Good manners stem from a heart that desires to help others, and the benefits of thoughtful behavior extend beyond yourself. Good manners impact even our society.

Good Manners Safeguard Against Selfishness

While selfishness breeds loneliness, damages reputations, and ruins relationships, appropriate manners protect against those conditions. You can only live a well-mannered life by caring about how you impact others with your actions and behavior. It is impossible to be selfish when you are mindful of others.

Good Manners Sparks Joy

You can feel joy when helping others. This deep satisfaction comes from knowing that your actions positively impact those around you. You can feel it, even when others seem not to notice. However, feel reassured that your good deeds will not go unnoticed by others.

We don't practice good manners just because we expect others to pay back for what we did. But regardless, it proves beneficial.

- You can't help to be good to people who are nice to you.
- You are more than willing to share with others when they are sharing something with you.
- When you help others, they are more likely to help you back.

Giving back may not have motivated you, but it could work to your advantage.

Good Manners can Keep you Motivated

Good manners make you feel good about being kind and generous to others. Feeling this inner contentment will help you maintain that calm and composed appearance even in a difficult situation. And because you feel good about yourself, it elevates your self-respect and keeps you motivated to do more good toward others.

Good Manners Impart Strength to Overcome Failure

You may experience failures from time to time, but when good manners and etiquette enhance your self-confidence, they provide you the inner strength to face challenges head-on, face disappointments, losses, and failures, accept criticisms, and move on. The same inner confidence will give you a positive mindset that enables you to maintain your composure, turn challenges into opportunities, weaknesses into strengths, and learn how to grow.

Good Manners Create Smoother Relationships

It is common for people to interact with those who are likable and cheerful rather than sad and unfriendly. However, practicing manners and good etiquette while you're young stops you from overreacting. You may feel empathy for these people at some point as good manners prevent resentment and create equal balance in relationships. They help you swallow your pride and be more considerate of the emotions of others.

FUNDAMENTALS OF TABLE MANNERS AND ETIQUETTE FOR TWEENS

You may face several challenges in your transition to adolescence, but equipping yourself with proper table manners and etiquette plays a significant role in creating a favorable impression during a social gathering.

Below you will find some basic table manners and etiquette to help you handle yourself on some occasions.

Simple Table Manners

Avoid crossing over others on the table when trying to reach for food or condiments. When passing for food, give it from left to right. Also, don't forget to say, "excuse me."

Pass both when someone asks for salt or pepper, even when they only ask for one.

When passing items, set them directly on the table instead of passing hand-to-hand, whether it be salt and pepper shakers, a butter plate, or a bread basket.

It would be best if you never took anything out of what's being passed en route to someone else.

Etiquette for Dining in a Restaurant

- As soon as seated, take the napkin, unfold it, and put it in your lap.

- Don't use the napkin to clean your nose, face, or cutlery.

- If you want to excuse yourself from the table, place the loosely folded napkin on either the left or right of your place. Never refold, or crumple it. Also, please don't leave it on the chair.

- After eating, semi-fold the napkin and leave it on the left side of the plate.

Etiquette for a Private Dinner Party

The meal starts at a private dinner party once the host or hostess unfolds their napkin. It signals you to do the same. Remember not to shake your napkin open. If it is a large napkin, spread it in half lengthwise.

The host or hostess again signals the end of the meal by placing their napkin on the table. When the meal is over, place your napkin to the left of your plate. Remember to refrain from wadding up or refolding your napkin.

WHY RESPECT IS IMPORTANT

In any relationship, respect is vital. Here are ways where you can show others you respect them.

How to Show Respect to Others

Step 1: Hear them out. If you want to show respect, listening to others is one of the best ways to attain your goal. However, listening to another who has an opposite point of view from yours could take a lot of work, but then, even just out of paying them respect, hear them out.

Step 2: Open your mind. Opening your mind toward others is also equivalent to respect. Even if you disagree with their perspective, at least you are willing to see what they are seeing in their light and be ready to learn from them.

Step 3: Be truthful. If you respect others, tell them the truth. Be honest about your feelings and opinions, even if you disagree with what they say.

Step 4: Consider their welfare. Consideration for others also means paying them respect. Also, consider their feelings and needs alongside yours. This includes making compromises or sacrifices. Do not just consider your own interests, but others' welfare as well.

Step 5: Respect their belongings. You don't give courtesy to people only. You must respect their time, property, and possessions. If you respect them, respect their belongings too. That way, they will feel the respect that you are giving them.

How to Deal With Disrespect From Others

Though you have no power over how other people would like to treat you, it's up to you how you'll handle disrespect when you face it.

Option 1: Ignore. If a person disrespects you, best to ignore it. Please don't give that person the attention they're seeking; don't interact or talk with them.

Option 2: Walk away. Walk away from disrespectful people if you can't bear to ignore them. It will surely relay the message that their behavior is not okay with you.

Option 3: Stand up for yourself. If you can't do option 1 or 2, here is option 3: Stand up for yourself. Be assertive in telling others that they are behaving unacceptably.

Option 4: Ask for help. Sometimes you need to ask for help when disrespect occurs. May it be a family member, a trusted friend, or even the authorities, when the situation arises, seek help when you can't manage it on your own.

In any relationship, paying respect is essential. A constructive social environment is created if you show others you respect them. However, if faced with disrespect, knowing how to deal with it is a great skill.

Consequences of Not Respecting Others

Respect others, and most probably, they will respect you too. Remember that it is a give-and-take relationship. Show respect first to gain it from others. Otherwise, disrespect in relationships will only result in all kinds of problems.

Conflict is a result of being disrespectful to other people. You will find yourself mostly in arguments and disputes if you disrespect others.

Another product of disrespect is social isolation. If you don't treat others with respect, for sure, they won't keep you company. Making and keeping friends will be challenging.

Be a model to those around you by setting a good example. Be honest, considerate, and open-minded.

A harmonious and constructive social environment can be created by respecting all people. Everyone can get positive outcomes from it.

The Benefits of Respecting Others

Improved relationships. Respect breeds improved relationships. People tend to mirror you when you pay them your respect. In turn, a positive and peaceful relationship will take place.

Less conflict. More respect equals less conflict. Respecting people will aid you in avoiding disputes and lead to a better social environment.

More socially connected. If you want to feel more connected socially, respect is the key. If you are a person who shows respect to everyone, more people will be attracted to keep you company. Making and keeping friends will not be a problem.

WHY DO YOU NEED TO HAVE SOCIAL SKILLS

What are Social Skills?

Social skills are behaviors and other forms of expression you need to create and maintain relationships effectively. They allow you to interact effectively and appropriately with others. Social skills include making friends, initiating conversations, communicating effectively, etc. They are mostly learned over time, beginning with your family and continuing throughout your life.

Learning social skills is vital for you as you grow and develop. They are highly associated with future success. Researchers have proven that youths who score higher on social skills measurements have four times the chance to graduate from an undergraduate course. Social skills are associated with independence, job success, and emotional well-being. With adaptive social skills, you can problem-solve, observe, and respond to social situations. Although many children naturally learn from social cues and behaviors, many still do not understand. Social skills will give you an advantage over other kids without such skills.

Why You Need to Have Social Skills

- There are certain milestones in childhood development that dictate growth and advancement. Having social skills is valuable in many areas of a child's life.

- Studies show that inadequate social skills can lead to poor results in child development. It can also prevent them from creating relationships and lead to loneliness, affecting their behavior, school performance, and adjustments. This is why it is essential to acquire social skills early in life.

- There are several social skills during child development, including:

- Sharing and cooperating

- Use of manners

- Using eye contact

- Understanding personal space

- Learning these skills will allow you to be successful in the future.

Children who are socially developed can form stronger friendships and have more chances to succeed in their education. Socially competent children will have the following benefits:

- Higher possibility of earning a high school diploma

- Twice as likely to attend post-secondary education

- Less likely to use illegal drugs

- Less likely to get into trouble

The Impact of Underdeveloped Social Skills

The lack of social skills in kids often leads to difficulties with relationships, isolation, depression, and anxiety. Lack of social skills in young kids is a matter of concern, like other developmental delays that could have negative effects in the future.

Shyness

Many kids are naturally shy and need help to get along with other kids. They are usually nervous and will often be quiet, and engaging in group activities is never a choice for them. Because they are not constantly exposed to other kids their age, they would rather trust adults.

Afraid of Getting Into Trouble

Kids who lack social skills often fear getting into trouble and choose not to stand out from the crowd or make decisions for themselves.

Bullying

Bullies often pick on kids who are not confident and less popular. Kids who lack social confidence fall victim to bullying.

Family Environment

Children brought up in a family where parents have trouble interacting with each other are less likely to develop social skills. Tensions and pressures in the home are more likely to hinder them from forming friendships.

HOW TO IMPROVE SOCIAL SKILLS

What to Do to Improve Social Skills?

Consider the following ways to improve your social skills:

Social Stories: Some stories can teach specific social skills that you may need clarification or help understanding. Being able to relate to the story will help you change some behavior or habit that needs to go.

Games: Playing any game with other kids will teach you not only about winning but also about losing in a game. This way, you will learn how to handle a losing situation in real life.

Play: Playing with other kids can help you develop joint attention, shared interests, cooperation, turn-taking, and appropriate games with toys.

Empathy: Practicing empathy will help you understand how others feel in certain situations. Learning to be in someone else's shoes is essential in your daily interaction with other kids and adults. For example, would you also laugh when you see someone laugh at others' mistakes? Having empathy will allow you to feel what that other kid must have thought at the moment and act on it. You may help that kid get away from the situation and show them your empathy, or you may reprimand other kids for laughing.

Activities to Help Improve Social Skills

Bean bag conversation:

- Sit with your friends, forming a circle.

- Give a topic or ask a question.

- Throw a bean bag, and the first one to catch the bean bag will contribute to the conversation.

After this, the bean bag is thrown again for someone to catch it.

Mirror: The mirror game will help you improve eye contact.

Singing: Singing will help you be aware of different emotions.

Turn-Taking: When playing turn-taking games like board games, say "my turn" or "your turn," as this will help you understand the importance of taking turns.

ACTIVITIES TO DEVELOP A POSITIVE MINDSET

Stress has been a regular part of our daily life. Everyone is vulnerable to stress—even you. In fact, you experience it at school, at home, or in a supermarket. One way to fight stress is to develop a positive mental attitude.

A positive mindset doesn't mean that you'll always have a smile pasted on your face or you only look cheerful. It pertains to an overall perspective in life. Since it's an attitude and mindset, you can develop it.

Here are six practical ways to accomplish this feat:

Activity #1: Practice Affirmations

Affirmations are encouraging and motivating statements. You can receive affirmations from your friends, parents, teachers, and loved ones. On the other hand, you can use affirmations to believe in yourself (e.g., "I can do it!").

For kids, affirmations usually involve scripted lines or mantras used in general or specific situations.

- General: "This will be a great day for me!"
- When you're nervous: "I can handle this!"
- When you're angry: "I am calm. I am in control."
- If you want to hurt somebody: "I am kind. My anger can't control me!"

The messages we send ourselves are vital to our happiness and general well-being. They affect our mindset as well as the people and things around us.

You can practice affirmations by . . .

- thinking out loud

- saying them with your inner voice

- saying them in front of the mirror

- writing them down in a booklet of affirmations

- using affirmation cards

- Example of affirmations:

I am strong.	I am beautiful no matter what others say.	I am kind.
My brain is powerful.	I am brave and confident.	I'm better than yesterday.
I am unique.	My feelings are valid.	I made mistakes, but I learned through them.

Activity #2: Stay Fit

Did you know that physical exercise can boost your mental prowess and help build your confidence? Exercising releases endorphins, the hormones that make you feel good. It reduces excess body fat and builds muscles, helping you develop a positive self-image. Moreover, physical activity keeps your brain healthy. This means you can think and understand more clearly, solve problems, and enjoy emotional balance.

Here are some workout ideas for you:

Activity #3: Record Moments

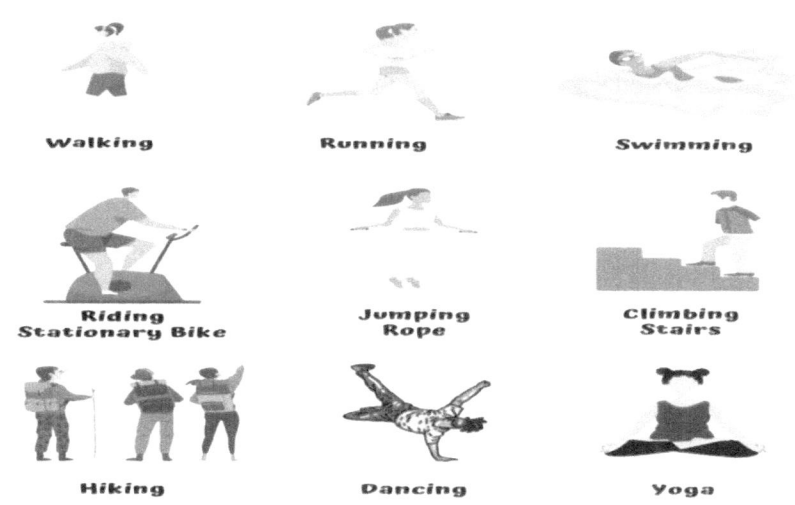

A person who can't often express their feelings and emotions misbehaves. Journaling is one of the most effective ways to process and externalize thoughts and emotions brewing inside you.

Journaling also motivates kids like you to pen down your goals. As you track down your accomplishments and milestones, you build your self-esteem. This simple activity, in turn, allows you to establish a positive mental attitude.

My Daily Journal

☼ ☁ ⛆ ❄   Date:

Another type of journal, the gratitude journal, involves logging everything you're thankful for. Keeping this type of diary helps improve your attitude and outlook in life.

A sample of a Gratitude Journal:

Gratitude Journal

s   m   t   w   t   f   s

Date :

Today Affirmation

Today i'm grateful for

Schedule

Hope

Note

Activity #4: Set and Achieve Goals

We talked about journaling your goals, but we will expand it in this activity.

Being a positive thinker alone doesn't make you an achiever. The very first step to your action is to set goals. Goal-setting helps you become more optimistic with a more profound sense of well-being. You're not merely staying put and wishing for the best. You have every intention to make those wishes come true.

In achieving those goals, you may experience setbacks that could negatively impact your outlook. Should this stop you? No.

Meeting obstacles or failing is normal. They are life's tests and can further develop your positive mental attitude.

To accomplish goals and develop life-long positive thinking, use the WOOP strategy:

THE WOOP STRATEGY	
Wish	Come up with the goal you want to achieve.
Outcome	Visualize the best possible outcome of achieving your goal. What would this result look like? How would you feel about this success?
Obstacle	Take all possible challenges that could prevent you from achieving your goal. Create a list of these obstacles and visualize each of them. Some of these

	hurdles may include distractions, such as playing video games until midnight, being on social media all the time, or a habit of procrastination.
Plan 	Create a strategy that will help you handle these obstacles effectively. For example, "I will put away my phone before studying, so I won't be tempted to check on my social media accounts and messages during my study."

Activity #5: Explore and Improve

Knowing your strengths allow you to develop them and experience breakthroughs that build your self-esteem. If you have fantastic math skills, join a club that caters to math wizards like you. If you're great at dancing, sign up for dance lessons.

Likewise, trying new things helps you gain a positive self-image. Exploring will introduce you to a lot of things that pique your interest. Ask your parents to guide you if you need help figuring out where to start.

Activity #6: Meditate

Experts believe meditation training focused on kindness and compassion improves physical, mental, and social well-being. This type of meditation triggers changes in a person's brain process associated with positive social behaviors. People who practice loving-kindness meditation tend to be more generous, mindful, and supportive.

In loving-kindness meditation, you think of your loved ones and send them positive thoughts. Later, you expand these thoughts to people you're acquainted with. For example, you think of your parents and say, "May you always feel happy. I always pray that you will always be healthy." You accustom your brain to be more optimistic by thinking or saying these positive thoughts.

HOW TO DEVELOP EMPATHY

What is Empathy?

Empathy is the ability to understand what others feel. It helps us to understand the following:

- The emotions and feelings of people
- Their motivations
- Their opinions and standpoints

Basically, empathy is putting yourself in another person's position to feel what they feel.

Empathy influences how we interact with the people around us. With empathy, you can understand why bullying and insulting others can be hurtful. At the same time, it teaches you how kindness and compassion bring out positive feelings and friendship.

How to Develop Empathy

Developing empathy allows you to perceive, reflect, and understand your behavior. It helps you discover and identify your feelings and convey them appropriately.

- **Talk about how you feel about things in life.** Discuss your emotions and feelings with your parents, friends, or loved ones. For example, you feel sad and angry because you saw a stranger kick a little dog. Telling someone about this experience can help you deal with if more effectively.

- **Observe and name what you see.** Notice the body language and non-verbal cues of people around you. Perhaps your mother bites her right thumbnail whenever she feels anxious, or your best friend's voice goes slightly higher when talking with her crush. Identifying and labeling these feelings will help you understand what others are going through.

- **Create empathy maps.** Choose a specific emotion or feeling. Imagine all your possible responses—what you may think, say, and do when you feel that way.

- **Help out at home.** This way, you will understand your parents and other family members. Doing simple chores will help you understand the challenges of others.

- **Volunteer.** Helping others develop kindness and compassion. It also enables you to interact with people from diverse backgrounds and circumstances.

- **Be Patient**. You can't develop empathy overnight or in just a few weeks. In fact, many adults haven't mastered this skill entirely! Empathy is a complex skill. It grows as you mature and put it into action.

Furthermore, developing these skills will help you better understand other people:

- Awareness of your own feelings and emotions
- Ability to manage feelings and emotions
- Acceptance of differences
- Ability to handle pressures and conflicts
- Ability to solve problems
- Respect for others
- Ability to obtain the things you need or want without hurting others

COLLABORATION SKILLS

Collaboration Skills and Why They Are Important

Collaboration and communication skills are held in high importance in the field of work. Even at present, people from across borders and from different walks of life work together. Students and job seekers looking for work in a global setting will be the usual standard in the near future. Therefore, you must harness these skills while you're still young.

Positive aspects of team-building skills include:
- Refining communication skills
- Developing critical thinking
- Building and establishing relationships
- Enhancing productivity and efficiency
- Developing leadership skills

- Being able to manage criticisms and use them constructively

Activities to Develop Collaboration

Meanwhile, here are some activities that will aid in boosting your collaboration skills:

Activity #1: Doing Creative Projects

Working for a common goal or task with individual units will improve your collaboration skills. You will also learn the advantages of productive communication.

Painting murals, filming short documentaries or videos, and producing stage plays are a few recreations where you can apply teamwork. You can also try collaborative writing, photo shoots, music recording, and website designing.

Activity #2: Camping

Camping is an incredible way to establish connections and build on collaboration skills in a fun and atypical setting. It also provides many opportunities to get to know the different sides of other people, especially if you're not too familiar with them. Maybe you would be surprised to know that your classmate John, who's usually shy and quiet, is a pro at setting up tents and cooking and how the straight-faced Jane can be humorous.

Activity #3: Organizing Scavenger Hunt for Teams

SCAVENGER HUNT

- ☐ something red
- ☐ things you bring in the mall
- ☐ something round
- ☐ things that have flowers
- ☐ two things that start with letter R
- ☐ something that glistens
- ☐ A book about friendship

This fun activity requires strategizing skills, communication skills, and teamwork. Participants can be grouped into teams with four to five members (depending on the number of participants). Each team receives a list of clues. Members have to work together to solve the clues and obtain the corresponding items. Of course, the fastest team to complete what is required ultimately wins.

Activity #4: Doing Community Projects

Brainstorm ideas with your team to identify what you can do for your community during your meetings. Post your goals and tasks in a bulletin for monitoring. You can also ask adults to support your team's endeavors.

Working together for a noble cause is one of the best ways to build a community while exercising empathy. You can improve your social and life skills while beautifying and cleaning the surroundings, designing the community garden, or organizing a fundraising event.

HOW TO MAKE FRIENDS EASILY

Wherever we go, we find friends. Whether you transfer to a new school or want to talk with other kids, it pays to have some essential skills. Here are ways to make friends easily, especially when you're the new kid.

Identify Someone Who Is A Potential Friend

Try looking around to see if there are friendly faces. Kids of your age usually share the same interest. See what they're doing and approach them by showing interest in their activity. You can start with kids in your class as you can have something in common. You can share notes or even share a snack during recess time.

If you're new to your community, look for other kids in the neighborhood. See where kids usually hang out. You may find them in the park, swimming pool, or skating rink, or you may join a community that interests you.

If you are good at acting, join the Drama Club or the school band or choir if you enjoy music. The most important thing is to take advantage of these friend-making activities.

Approach People You Want to Know

You may communicate well through verbal communication. However, you should also be aware of how you communicate non-verbally. Most of the time, your body language relays a lot of information, and if you learn to communicate through your body language, it could be more effective in gaining a friend.

For example, smiling could show other kids you are friendly and want to join them. Maintaining eye contact is essential when approaching a kid you want to make friends with. It should be that you are interested in them. You may drop a quick compliment if you want to start a conversation, for example:

- What a beautiful dress you have!

- That's quite awesome for a scooter!

- You've got a cute doggie for a pet!

Asking a question helps you catch someone's attention. Try asking something such as the following:

- Do we belong to the same class?

- Are you also in this club?

- May I take a look at your notes?

228

You may not feel confident in finding a friend or approaching one. Many people also lack the confidence to start a conversation with anyone they don't know. Realizing this could help you gain the courage to talk to a stranger.

Nurturing Friends

To have long-lasting friendships, you must get to know them more. You can develop a friendships spending time with others. For example, you may invite them to your home, and they will also invite you to visit theirs. You will become closer as you frequently visit each other's homes and meet your families.

Communication skills are essential in every relationship. It's a two-way process, just as friendship gives and takes. If you want to keep your friends, listen and not simply hear what they say. It is essential to show that you are interested in them and the things they do and say.

Also, let your friends know what you want. Remember that friendship gives and takes. As you allow them to express themselves freely without interruption, they must listen to you when it is time for you to speak. You must be able to express yourself in every way.

Friendships are nurtured when friends share ideas and experiences. When you trust your friend, and they trust you, you can start sharing experiences and even secrets without worrying that they will let them out. But do this only after years of being friends. It will be hard for any of you if you will experience being betrayed.

Empathy is an essential ingredient of a long-lasting friendship. You have to be sensitive to other people's emotions just as they are to yours. Friends don't want to hurt each other. If they do so, they immediately find ways to settle the disagreement.

What It Means to have a Good Friend

Friendships give you a sense of belonging, boost confidence, make it easier to avoid unhealthy lifestyles, reduce stress, and help you through tough times. But how can you cultivate friendships? Here's how you can gain good friends.

A good friendship can make you feel good. By saying nice things to each other and giving compliments, friends lift each other. You should feel good about yourself and help your friend feel good.

Good friends support each other. We all have different habits and interests. You should remain open even if your friend's interests do not align with yours. Try their interest and see if you like them. If not, try to encourage each other as friends understand even when they have separate interests.

Be a good listener. In a healthy friendship, both parties are interested in what the other has to say. So, listen and refrain from interrupting when your friend is speaking.

Be trustworthy. Never share your friend's secrets. Maintain trust between you and never be judgmental.

Respect Boundaries. Even if you are close for a long time, there are lines you must not go over. When issues arise, be ready to work through such cases to settle the problem. The same with your friend if he happens to go beyond your boundary.

Give your time. Making great friendships involves time and effort. By giving them your time, you let them into your life. The more time you spend with each other, the more comfortable you become.

Equal Connection. Being a friend doesn't just mean listening to each other. In real friendship, no one is dominant as it is a mutual relationship. You must be able to lift each other and make each other feel good.

Create a community. Although certain connections can feel special, like when you have someone you call a best friend, having more than one friend in your life is beneficial and healthy. It can widen your perspective and expose you to different types of friendships while expanding your support network.

Quality over quantity. While you can have as many friends in your social media community, you can still feel pressure. Resist this pressure and pay attention to quality connections that come with having many superficial friends.

HOW TO HANDLE CRITICISMS

Criticism or judgment can hurt your ego, but you need to handle it. Constructive criticism is a feedback method that provides valuable, specific, and actionable suggestions aimed at helping. Positively viewing criticism can help you focus on improving your performance and work attitude instead of seeing it as a negative comment that destroys you.

Here are ways to help you manage objections.

Test Yourself

Consider the following scenarios to test yourself:

#1 —Your friends tell you to study more, not hang out with bad influences.

Reject it: She's just jealous because I have other friends.

Accept it: She's right, as my grades are lower than before.

#2 —Your mother tells you not to spend much time on social media.

Reject it: I'm not spending much time. Are two hours too long?

Accept it: I better listen to mom.

#3 —Your teacher tells you that you could have done better on your essay if you had focused on your main idea.

Reject: She always has a comment.

Accept it: It's good to follow her advice.

If you cannot take constructive criticism, you miss getting all the benefits! Accepting constructive criticism is an important skill you need to learn, as it will serve you well now and in your adult life.

WHY DO YOU NEED CONSTRUCTIVE CRITICISM?

We all make mistakes; no one is perfect. To correct our errors, we need someone to correct us when we go wrong, as our mistakes are often not visible to our eyes. However, remember that we all have imperfections and that making mistakes is a part of our life. If you want to do good, learn to listen to what others say to avoid making the same mistake repeatedly.

By listening to constructive criticism, you can do better next time.

HOW YOU CAN ACCEPT CONSTRUCTIVE CRITICISM

To learn to accept constructive criticisms, you must . . .

Listen. Learn to listen when someone is criticizing you for the better. Don't get defensive and interrupt the person giving advice. Just relax and learn from the corrections. Next time you will do better.

Hear the message. When your ego is hurt, you might be tempted to get back on your critic and point out their flaws. But it won't help you to get angry. Instead, listen, as there is always truth to the criticism. Take advantage of the message even if you dislike the messenger and don't want to hear them criticizing you. You may feel offended, but when you listen to the message, you may soon realize its truth.

Have a balanced view of yourself. Just because you were criticized does not mean that you're a failure. It simply means that, like all the rest, you have your fair share of flaws. Even the one giving you those criticisms is exempted from this, but be thankful that you were allowed to see these imperfections so you can improve them.

Set a goal for improvement. Once you accept criticism, you can overcome your defensive behavior and start correcting what was wrong based on the advice given. Set your goal and create an action plan to follow your progress. Once you can deal with your criticisms, you have learned to be honest and accept your flaws. Only when you have accepted that you're not perfect will you be able to think of ways to improve.

The bottom line is to recognize that we need to learn from one another, and constructive criticism is a tool you will need to polish as you grow older.

Practicing good manners is essential when dealing with different types of people. And because social interaction is a part of your daily life, success depends on building relationships and connections. Learning about good manners and social skills is a must. Social skills are effective in creating and maintaining relationships, and observing good manners is essential to social skills.

CHAPTER 7

GOAL-SETTING AND DECISION-MAKING SKILLS

"A person should set his goals as early as he can and devote all his energy and talent to getting there. With enough effort, he may achieve it. Or he may find something that is even more rewarding. But in the end, no matter what the outcome, he will know he has been alive."
— Walt Disney

Setting goals is important when you make plans to achieve something in life. They help you to continue challenging yourself to do your best toward achieving results. While you set your goals early and devote all your energy and talent to achieving what you want, you may acquire it and even be rewarded more than you expect. Sometimes, it will be different from what you want, but regardless of the result, you have tried your best.

WHY SETTING GOAL IS GOOD FOR YOU

If you want to do something big, setting your goal is one of the most critical actions. It is necessary to know how important goal setting is and apply this knowledge. Understanding the following benefits could be the starting point to achieving your life goals.

A goal helps you focus. With a plan, you can focus on every step, enabling you to move in the right direction. Since the body follows what the mind dictates, setting a goal helps you stay focused and motivated. Be sure to be aware of why you should take specific actions and where these actions lead you.

Goals allow you to measure progress. As you do each task, you can measure your progress by setting your goals, as there is always a definite endpoint to make a comparison. You have to write down your plan to visualize your progress and note the objectives you have achieved in every step. It will motivate you to achieve your goal fast.

Goals can help you avoid procrastination. With every goal set, you have the responsibility to achieve it. You must complete each task by taking steps without delay.

Goals are rewarding. You can feel satisfaction every time you can achieve your goal. On the other hand, unfulfilled goals can be frustrating, resulting in stress which can slow down your personal growth.

Goals-setting contributes to self-improvement. Well-defined goals can improve your performance in all areas of life. However, rewards will depend on your efforts to achieve those goals.

Goals can motivate you to achieve more. Knowing what you want to achieve and conveying it through your plan can encourage you to go in the desired direction and understand how to go there. It provides you the motivation and the desire to move fast in setting a new goal.

Goals make the road easier. Setting bigger goals can be time-consuming. But you can quickly solve this by setting smaller goals. Dividing complex and bigger goals into small chunks can be easier to attain, and it is clear what action you should work on first. By committing to smaller daily goals, you will soon achieve the bigger ones.

HOW TO SET GOALS

Grow Your Hobby and Set a Goal to Achieve Success

You will always find it interesting to do something you like, such as your hobby. You can grow your hobby by setting your goal. A hobby is easier to achieve because you have the interest and passion you have practiced for a long time.

You Must Own this Goal

Once you set a goal, it must be yours, not anyone else's. Developing your plan involves thinking about your personal and intellectual strengths. You have your own goal because you want to achieve your dreams.

Know Your Limit

Setting your goal can be challenging, and you must understand your limits. Achieving your goal must fall within your limit, as going beyond can lead to failure.

Set Goals in Stages

To avoid getting overwhelmed, set your goal in three stages:

- Short-term
- Mid-Term

- Long-Term

Connect your short-term goal to your long-term goal. Short-term goals are based on a daily, weekly, or month.

A medium-term goal takes longer. You can achieve it in more than a month, six months, or less than a year. Mid-term goals remind you of your long-term goal.

A long-term goal takes longer, and you can achieve your long-term goal in a year, three years, or more. Long-term goals are essential and are your life goals.

Write Down Your Ideas, Breaking Then Into Smaller Chunks

When making big dreams, you must start small. Writing down your goals can make them more realistic as you will have a blueprint of your target. You can decide what tasks are necessary to achieve your goal. Write down all these tasks and give a deadline for each task. Also, write down all your ideas even if you think they could be better. As you go along, you will learn what among these ideas works and which are impossible. What is important is realizing that your ideas, no matter how small, can help you achieve big goals.

Making the Journey Beautiful

Achievement of your goal may take time. But as you're on your journey to achieving your plan, you will learn something from it. There is always a 50-50 chance of failure and success, but try to think so you can enjoy your journey positively. Be patient on your journey to make it beautiful. A beautiful journey is more likely to increase its chance of success. In between achieving your goal, add fun activities.

SET SMART GOALS

GOALS

S pecific

M easurable

A ttainable

R elevant

T ime-bound

When setting your goal, make sure it's SMART. Here's what a SMART GOAL looks like.

It's **Specific**. Anyone can easily understand what you want to achieve. Because it is clearly defined and easy to understand, anyone can help if needed.

It's **Measurable**. It's easy to target when there's measurement involved. Saying that you want to save $100 by the month is better than just saying you want to save by the end of the month.

It's **Attainable**. Your goal must be achievable. For example, saying you intend to save a million dollars by the end of the year is not achievable. If you are still a student, you can't achieve this goal. Anyone can easily see that your goal is not attainable.

It's **Relevant**. Your goal must always have something to do with you. How can you achieve its goal when your plan falls outside your interest? You will never have the motivation to do something that has no relevance to you at all.

It's Timely. Be able to set a reasonable deadline for your goal. You can focus and work towards achieving your goal once there is a deadline.

HOW TO REACH YOUR GOALS

To keep you focused on achieving your goal, follow these simple steps.

Write Down Your Goal	
Set a deadlines	
Work on your mindset	
Develop your skill set	
Take the first step	

| Continue to completion | |
| Reward Yourself | |

WHY HAVING GOOD DECISION-MAKING SKILLS IS IMPORTANT IN ACHIEVING YOUR GOALS

Even though making decisions is sometimes scary, doing so is simple when there are clear-cut actions to take.

Nobody has excellent inborn decision-making abilities. It is a talent that is developed. This means that the more decisions you make, the better you will become at them. It's tricky to master because the more you become skilled at making decisions, the more complex the challenges you'll encounter.

Some people become anxious when making important decisions because they worry they will choose poorly. The foundation of decision-making is this. Any time you have a choice between two options, there is always a chance that you will choose the "better" or "worse" option. For example, if you are trying to decide whether to study or not, think about what the consequences of that decision will be to determine which option is better. If you study, you may do well on the test (that is the better option).

Some decisions are more difficult, however. Deciding whether to report bullying involves more planning than simple choices like whether to study or what shoes to wear.

Remember that many decisions you'll need to make don't have to be right or wrong. You will have to decide based on how you know yourself, your circumstances, your requirements, your preferences, and what you believe will be best for you. Here are eight steps you may take to help you make difficult decisions.

Steps to Making Good Decisions

#1 — **Know what issue you face.** Determine what problem you need to resolve. Write it so you can be clear with your goals. List the reasons you have to fix this problem. This stage point provides some insight into the importance of your decision.

#2 — **Gather information and request guidance.** What you need to learn, put in writing. Interview individuals, such as other students who were present or have experienced the problem. What can others say about this? For example, imagine you are trying to decide whether to take an after school job. Assemble data from reliable sources (e.g., ask your school counselor about how many hours per week school requires and how many hours per week a part-time job requires). Which facts apply? What is preventing you (such as believing that you can't manage both, bad habits, a fear of taking on too much responsibility, etc.)? With this step, you can gain both objective (unbiased) and subjective (biased) information.

#3 — **What matters most to you?** Describe your values (honesty, good grades, independence, money, etc.). What factors (such as the viewpoint of your family) do you want your decision to reflect?

#4 — **Brainstorm and list all of your potential choices.** Consider options. (For example, work five, ten, or twenty hours a week, don't work, take on a job during summer only, etc.).

#5 — **What are the results of each decision (both positive and negative)?** To evaluate the pros and cons of each option provided in step 4, you can use steps 2 and 3. Write all your data in a table.

#6 — **Select the option that is best for you.** After you complete the stages above, this becomes much simpler. Rank your choices, if necessary. Rank the items in order using your research. If you need to, take a few days to reflect before returning to the problem.

#7 — Make a plan and execute it. Once you've decided, make a strategy outlining the specific actions you'll take. Put your plan into action.

#8 — Analyze the outcomes. This can only be done after you've made your choice, followed through with your plan, and received feedback (e.g., your report card and regular pay). What would you say about your choice? How did the actions you took go? Are you still fulfilling your priorities? What lessons have you taken away? It is a crucial action for improving your ability to make decisions. Use everything you've learned to go back to the drawing board and reassess your choices if you realize they didn't turn out well the first time. If your choice were not the best, it would not be the end for you. Retrace your steps and begin where you think is a good starting point.

Goal-setting helps you to strive for achievement. Although it can be challenging, it increases your efficiency and effectiveness by targeting specific outcomes, giving you a higher chance of success. Learning to make good decisions enables you to make better choices to achieve your goal.

CHAPTER 8

BECOMING THE BEST VERSION OF YOURSELF

"It's not selfish to love yourself, take care of yourself, and make your happiness a priority. It's necessary." – Mandy Hale

Learning self-care is essential for everyone, especially at a young age. It prepares you for adulthood as you grow and develop physically, mentally, and emotionally. You become aware of your different needs, and learning the importance of taking care of yourself can help lessen stress, improve relationships, and promote overall wellness.

Self-care is ensuring you can take care of yourself to help you manage your stress. When you are relaxed, well-nourished, and cared for, it will be easier for you to help others.

It can be surprising, but self-care can be highly beneficial to you.

- You will learn to identify your physical and emotional needs and can therefore take care of those needs.

- Practicing self-care at a young age will create a foundation that will benefit you later as an adult.

- It will develop your healthy habits.

- You will become more independent and understand how to care for yourself.

- You will develop the skills necessary to keep yourself physically, mentally, and emotionally.

WHAT IS SELF-CARE?

Self-care is taking the time to do things for yourself that help you live well and improve your physical and mental well-being. Regarding mental health, self-care can help you handle stress, increase your energy, and lower your risk of illnesses. Even small self-care activities in your daily life can have a significant impact.

TAKING GOOD CARE OF YOUR BODY

During the tween stage (8-12 years old), you may experience changes in your body, affecting your self-esteem, confidence, lifestyle, and hygiene. This stage is what we call the "tween" period. While going through such a stage, taking care of your body is essential to ensure that you are prepared for puberty and will adapt well to the physical changes your body will undergo.

Maintain Good Hygiene

Good personal hygiene is integral to keeping your body healthy. A good example is the simple act of washing your hands before eating and after using the toilet. These are proven effective ways of fighting off germs and avoiding sickness. Once you start the puberty stage, there are changes in your body that require you to focus more on your hygiene. Here are ways to ensure you're on track with keeping your body clean.

- Wash your hands before and after each meal.
- Take a bath every day.
- Change your clothes regularly and after physical activity.
- Change underwear and other clothes are worn next to the skin often.
- Make sure to brush and floss your teeth after meals and visit your dentist regularly.

- Clean your feet and dry them well before putting on socks to avoid smelly feet. Use cotton socks instead of those made of synthetic fibers.

- Keep your fingernails short and clean.

Have a Skincare Routine to Prevent Acne

- Acne is common in kids during puberty and can be a form of blackheads, pimples, whiteheads, or cysts. If your parents have acne during their teens, you are also more likely to have acne. To prevent and treat acne, follow this skincare routine.

- Wash your face at least twice daily with a mild cleanser and warm water. Gently massage the cleanser into your face with your fingertips. Avoid scrubbing, picking, or scratching your skin. Also, avoid astringents, as they can dry out and irritate your skin. Instead, use a light, water-based moisturizer with SPF 15 or higher. It can protect your skin from the sun and prevent it from drying.

- If you wear makeup, choose water-based products that are non-allergenic or non-comedogenic. Clean your face and remove your makeup before going to bed using makeup remover. If you have severe acne, see a dermatologist. The earlier you address it, the faster it will go away. You can avoid scars on your face and body because of acne.

Use Deodorants for Odor Control

As soon as you reach puberty, a new type of sweat gland develops in sensitive areas like the armpits. Bacteria favor feeding on the sweat this type of gland produces, leading to body odor. Washing your body and changing clothes as often as possible will prevent the build-up of bacteria and avoid body odor. It is a good time for you to start using antiperspirant deodorant. Apply deodorants under your arms, especially if you sweat a lot after physical activity. This is to avoid the strong odor from the sweat glands in your armpits.

Take good care of your hair

Dust and oil can build up in your hair and scalp. You must wash your hair to help control oil build-up, which may cause dandruff and skin irritation.

Shampoo your hair regularly. Avoid scrubbing, scratching, and rubbing your scalp and hair. Use conditioner after shampooing to keep it hydrated and healthy. If you have dandruff, use anti-dandruff products to control it. When using styling gels and lotions, ensure that you use products appropriate for your hair texture.

Shave your body hair once it grows

Different parts of your body may grow hair, including arms, legs, and armpits. When you are ready, you may shave any unwanted hair in any part of your body, although at this stage, you are most likely to grow fine hair that you don't need to remove at all. However, if you really need to remove them, you may ask your parents to show you how to do it, as you do not want to hurt yourself.

If you need to shave armpit or leg hair, use shaving gel or warm water and soap to create a lather when shaving your armpit hair. Also, use a razor made for body hair. Armpit hair may grow in different directions, so you must shave in different directions.

Boys develop later than girls, and hair growth may start showing up, but you do not need to shave. However, for a cleaner look, have your hair trimmed regularly.

HOW TO STAY HEALTHY

How Does the Body Use Energy?

Your body uses energy to function and grow. It takes energy from calories in food and drinks. To stay healthy, you need to balance the energy you take in from food and beverages with the energy you use for growth and functioning. Keeping your energy in balance helps you stay healthy and fit.

People differ in the number of calories they need daily. Factors affecting your required calorie intake are:

- Genes
- Weight
- Height
- Age
- Activities

Choose Healthy Foods and Drinks

To eat healthily, you must be able to control how much and the type of food to eat. Replace foods with high sugar, salt, and unhealthy fats with whole grains, vegetables, low-fat protein food, and low-fat or fat-free dairy foods.

Vegetables and Fruits

Half of your plate must contain fruits and vegetables. Orange, red, and dark green vegetables are enriched with Vitamin C, fiber, and calcium. Adding spinach, tomatoes, and other greens to your sandwich will give you more veggies.

Grains

Whole grains like brown rice, whole-wheat bread, oatmeal, and whole-grain cereals are more nutritious than refined-grain, white rice, and white bread.

Dairy

Products like fat-free or low-fat milk and yogurt help build strong bones and teeth. If you are lactose intolerant or can't digest lactose, the sugar in milk can cause stomach pain or gas. Choose lactose-free milk or soy milk with added calcium.

Fats

Your body needs fat to grow and develop while keeping your hair and skin healthy, but fats carry more calories in every gram than carbs and protein. Some of these fats aren't healthy. Some fats that are liquid and come from plants are healthy fats, including oils from avocados, seeds, nuts, and olives. Some seafood, such as tuna and salmon, also contain healthy oils. As much as possible, avoid solid fats like lard, margarine, and butter as they often have saturated and trans fats which are unhealthy. Foods containing saturated fats are cheese, fatty meats, and dairy products made from whole milk. Fried chicken, fries, and cheeseburgers also have trans and saturated fats.

Minimize your Sodium Intake

Your daily requirement for sodium, often found in salt, is minimal. You need no more than a teaspoon of sodium in a day. Too much sodium content can be unhealthy as it increases your blood pressure and puts you in danger.

Processed food in cans or packages has more sodium than fresh fruits and vegetables. Try using herbs and spices for seasoning your foods, and always read the label to know how much sodium there is.

Limit Your Sugar

Some foods have natural sugar, while ice cream, goodies, and other desserts have added sugar. Sugars have added calories but no vitamins and fibers. Lower your sugar intake to stay healthy in body shape and weight.

Control Food Portions

Consuming more than needed can keep you out of balance. A food portion is the amount of food you consume at one time.

When consuming fast food, choose healthier or smaller portions. Opt for salad or lean meats instead of fried chicken or fries.

Don't Skip Meals

Skipping meals can lead you to gain more weight as you eat more later to make up for the missed meal. So instead of cutting, consider the following:

- Eat breakfast every day.

- Have packed lunch on school days.

- Eat dinner with the family.

- Join in grocery shopping and meal planning at home.

EXERCISE IS GOOD FOR YOU

Physical activity pertains to any bodily movement that requires spending energy. It involves daily activities, regular fitness exercises, and organized sports. Physical activities are also categorized according to intensity:

- Light: everyday activities, such as strolling, cooking, washing dishes, and dusting.

- Moderate: activities that make you tired slightly. They include jogging, brisk walking, biking, dancing, and hiking.

- Vigorous: activities that can increase your heart rate and breathe heavily. They include playing games or sports, running, swimming, skipping, and some forms of dance.

Moderate and vigorous exercises such as jumping, climbing, running, and running can strengthen your bones and muscles. Squats, lunges, and push-ups can also help you achieve this feat.

Aside from strengthening your bones and muscles, doing regular physical activities is necessary because . . .

- it helps you develop good posture.

- it improves your immune system and cardio-respiratory fitness.

- it helps you control weight, lowering your risk for obesity, type-2 diabetes, and heart disease.
- it reduces your risk for anxiety and depression.

Physical activities can also help you to . . .

- improve your focus and concentration.
- break long hours of studying and being stationary.
- lower stress levels.
- boost your self-esteem and confidence.
- building social skills.

How Much Physical Activity Do You Need?

Tweens like you should do moderate-to-vigorous physical activities for at least an hour daily. The following goals will help you design the ideal exercise regimen that suits your lifestyle:

- To strengthen bones
- To strengthen muscles
- To boost cardiovascular fitness

Balancing Homework and Physical Activities

You can do any of these activities in between homework tasks or during breaks for 10 minutes. When you need about 60 minutes a day for physical activities for balance, you can distribute them throughout the day, depending on your number of breaks. You may have three of these exercises if you have two intervals. For example, perform 10 minutes of stretching, 10 minutes of sit-ups, and another 10 minutes of push-ups for your first break. Then, for your second break, you can do 10 minutes of jumping jacks, 10 minutes of squats, and 10 minutes of lunges. The key idea is to fill your 60-minute physical activity requirements throughout the day.

- Stretching exercises
- Push-ups
- Jumping jacks
- Squats
- Lunges
- Sit-ups

Balancing Physical Activities and Screen Time

While using your electronic devices, you must also be aware of creating a balance between physical activities and screen time. It's easy to pass the time watching the screen, but you don't need to be stationary. Do exercises that can provide you an opportunity to move as well, like:

- Use video dance games instead of playing mobile games.
- Take photos of beautiful scenery using your phone camera.

- Take videos while you're dancing. Replay it later to monitor your technique and note what you must improve.

Physical Activity for Tweens With Additional Needs

Physical activity can be equally crucial and challenging for kids with additional needs. If you are one of these kids, keep going, as many organized activities have been modified and supported to help you keep going. Some playgrounds are even designed and built with special equipment and sensory equipment.

Ask your parents to check if there are available support groups and sporting organizations in your local area. Your family could also take time to think of some activities that fit your needs and do them with you. Outdoor physical activity is essential as you can get the Vitamin D you need for strong bones and muscles while helping you build your movement skills.

You can do some easy exercises that don't require gym fees and special equipment and you can do at home. A little reminder though— you must ask your parents or doctor if they suit you.

Chair Squats

Sit-Backs

Butterfly Breath

Jump Rope

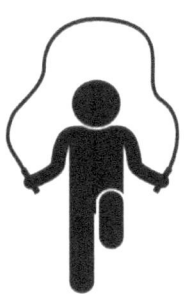

Dance

Trampoline

MAKE SLEEP A PRIORITY

Sleep is essential to maintaining a healthy lifestyle as a tween. Having eight to ten hours of quality sleep helps your growth, development, and well-being. It allows you to enjoy doing things with your family and friends. It also lets you do your activities, passions, and hobbies.

Setting up a sleep schedule is essential to create a regular sleep pattern and to not disrupt your body clock. Going to bed and waking up early on a regular schedule can help you avoid napping in the morning. Snoozing can easily throw off your internal clock.

Before going to bed at night, have some relaxing moments with yourself. Reading a book, taking a cool or hot bath, or drinking a cup of hot milk can ease your body tension buildup for the day. Shut off-screen time. You have spent enough time with your gadgets like cell phone, tablet, laptop, or desktop computer the whole day. You don't need to extend your viewing hours inside your bedroom, even with the television.

Set up your bedroom for a comfortable night's sleep. It must be calm, quiet, and with minimal light. If you're comfortable listening to soothing music, you may have it while you crawl under your favorite blanket or comforter.

CHOOSING WHAT TO WEAR

For Tween Girls

It can be challenging to decide what to wear, where to shop, and when to wear certain clothes. Follow the steps ahead to understand how to survive this transition into adolescence.

Plan your outfit a day in advance. Take time to ponder over what you will do that day. Are you going to school or staying at home? Whatever you're doing that day should have an impact on your decision. If it's pouring rain, you want to avoid being stuck in shorts all day.

Examine your closet. Look through your wardrobe to see what you have available to wear. If you don't like or don't fit some of your clothes, you may donate them to a local charity or sell them at a garage sale.

Feel comfortable. Choose something that appeals to you. Wear something that makes you feel at ease. When shopping, buy something you will think of wearing and not just keep it in your wardrobe. Some girls would buy clothes because they are fashionable, only to find out later that they did not wear them well. Make sure to wear something you want and not because they look good on models.

Accept that your body is changing.

Everyone's body changes as they get older. Going up a size or two could indicate that you're growing taller or that your hips are becoming broader. If something doesn't fit, don't worry about it; instead, get it in a larger size or go to a teen store.

Dress in age-appropriate attire. To appear more mature, you don't need to buy 5-inch (12.7 cm) heels or super-short skirts. Have fun with your style while remaining true to yourself.

Be self-assured. Clothing is one of the most effective ways to express yourself. You may show people how you feel, with writings on a t-shirt or a funny picture on comfy clothes. However, the primary goal is to make you feel more confident and genuinely recognize the beautiful woman you are.

For Tween Boys

Are you tired of wearing the same old clothes that you've had for years? You may not be fashionable, but you must develop your own style. It may take some time and work, but understanding your body type can help you upgrade your style and be a stylish young man.

Develop Your Style

Get the Basics. Get the best of what you have. You don't have to buy new stuff to be stylish. What is important is knowing how to match your clothes.

Get the right fit. Make sure all your clothes fit you correctly and make you feel comfortable. Some clothes will serve you better depending on your height, weight, and body structure. Avoid horizontal stripes in favor of vertical ones if you're a bigger guy. Vertical lines will draw the viewer's attention downward and make you look more fit.

Keep your personality the same to fit in with what's popular. Changing to a particular style or because it's trendy doesn't mean it's right for you.

Wear cute shoes. Make sure that your shoes are comfortable to wear.

Update Your Wardrobe

Update your wardrobe to reflect current fashion trends. Being fashionable necessitates some creative alterations. Experiment with new looks and avoid anything that makes you uncomfortable. Updating your closet can seem daunting and quickly get pricey, which can be difficult, especially if you're still growing and don't have much money.

Divide your clothes into categories: those you like and wear and those you don't. Clear out your closet by donating or selling items you no longer wear. Then examine your "keep" pile. Note which clothes are in style and which ones aren't. It will assist you in establishing a foundation for your updated wardrobe.

Plan a shopping trip. Ask your parents, older sibling, girlfriend, or any knowledgeable friend to accompany you when

LIFE SKILLS FOR TWEENS

shopping. They can give you good advice and help you choose some great clothes. Your siblings or peers will be able to provide tips on what works or doesn't work for you or pick out something that you might need help with.

Give away any clothes you no longer wear. Make a list of the clothing items you'll need as staples. For example, you may want one pair of jeans for almost any occasion, a couple of chinos, a dress shirt, a sweater, and a casual button-down shirt. Often we hang onto clothes that don't fit or we hardly ever wear. Collect these clothes, donate them to a charity, or sell them via a garage sale.

Mix and Match. If you're going to school, you should wear clothes you'll feel comfortable in all day. You can also put together several fashionable looks with a few key pieces, such as a dark pair of jeans. You can wear it with sneakers, a sweater to school, a blazer or light jacket, and change into boots for after-school activities. You'll create a new look in a few minutes by adding or changing a few items. Depending on your mood, mix and match items. Perhaps you're in a street-style mood rather than a classy mood. Wear sneakers with jeans or joggers, a simple t-shirt, and a light jacket.

Cleaning Up Your Look

Accent your wardrobe with accessories. Minor additions to your wardrobe will go a long way toward elevating your style. Consider wearing something that can serve as your signature, such as a scarf, hat, bracelet, etc. Remember that fashion is subjective, and the number of accessories you wear should make you feel at ease. Look for sentimental accessories, such as a necklace, that you already own. You don't need to buy them, or if you do, they don't need to be costly.

Make sure that you wear the right shoes to complete your outfit. While you can wear a pair of shoes with multiple outfits, some are inappropriate for every occasion. You want to avoid showing up to a formal event wearing skater shoes. Wearing nicer shoes with a casual outfit is always easier than wearing sneakers with a dressier one.

Groom yourself. Clothing that fits well and looks good will only take you so far. To be fashionable includes taking good care of your own body. Whether you like long, buzz cut, or somewhere in the middle, consider adding some product to make it look styled rather than unkempt. Also, remember to wash it regularly.

Keep your nails clean. Dirty or long nails are never appealing and can give an untidy impression that you don't care about your appearance.

Loving and taking care of yourself is a necessity in life. These are essentials to make life better and happier for you. They are why you need to learn and acquire self-care skills and create the best version of yourself.

CONCLUSION

Building the necessary life skills should start at an early age. It's like establishing the foundation. When you grow up without foundation, you will always struggle to cope with frustrations, disappointments, sadness, and other challenging emotions that may lead to an emotional breakdown and loss of hope. On the other hand, if you start learning essential life skills now, you can rest assured that you will be a strong, resilient, and happy individual.

Learning essential life skills will help you cope with everyday challenges and prepare you for a brighter tomorrow. Your actions and choices today will indeed have an impact on your future. Doing it right at the start will make your journey to the end more manageable and less stressful.

Now that you're fully equipped with the different life skills, start practicing them and set yourself up for success!

LEAVE A REVIEW

If you found this book helpful and think that it could help others like you who are trying to gain their life skills at a young age, please consider leaving a review. Your kind words can help other tweens find the resource they need. I'd be super grateful to your review!

LEAVE A REVIEW

REFERENCES

Child Passenger Safety: Get the Facts | Transportation Safety | CDC. (n.d.). https://www.cdc.gov/transportationsafety/child_passenger_safety/cps-factsheet.html

Concussions.(2018).Kidshealth.org. https://kidshealth.org/en/parents/concussions.html

Corners, E. (2023.) *Study skills guide: Study tips, strategies & lessons for students.* Study Skills Guide: Study Tips, Strategies & Lessons. https://www.educationcorner.com/study-skills.html

Helmets - a risk factor that can save young lives! - Road Safety - a global issue facing young people. - Yours. (n.d.). http://www.youthforroadsafety.org/road-safety/helmets

Hepler, L. (2018, August 3). *Cardiopulmonary Resuscitation (CPR).* Healthline; Healthline Media. https://www.healthline.com/health/first-aid/cpr

Johnston, I. (2004, October 1). *Reducing injury from speed-related road crashes*. Injury Prevention. https://injuryprevention.bmj.com/content/10/5/257

Road safety. (n.d.). PAHO/WHO | Pan American Health Organization. https://www.paho.org/en/topics/road-safety

Speed management: Why is speed such a crucial road safety issue? – Making Traffic Safer. (2018, May 2). https://making-traffic-safer.com/speed-management-why-is-speed-such-crucial-road-safety-issue/

When a Child Is Choking (Age 1 to 12 Years). (n.d.). Saint Luke's Health System. https://www.saintlukeskc.org/health-library/when-child-choking-age-1-12-years